SEVERN TANKING

B. A. LANE

Designed Produced and Published by
Douglas McLean

at

The Forest Bookshop
8 St John Street, Coleford, Glos. GL16 8AR

Printed in Great Britain by
Billing and Son Ltd., Worcester

ISBN 0 946252 23 8

Chapter One

The Start of my Interest in the River

I was first taken to sea by my parents at the age of two. This was in 1926 on board a steam and sail collier, the 'SS Seaforth' of Bristol. I was later told by my mother that this was when a film crew had taken over the ship to film scenes for Treasure Island, off Fowey in Cornwall. I was also as a child, taken along on the trips to France and Belgium to deliver coal, or sometimes to stand by the fishing fleet off the Shetland Isles. In those days trawlers were all coal fired, so they were loaded with steam coal in South Wales at Cardiff, Barry and Swansea and then they sailed North to the fishing fleet, and bunkered whichever trawler requested coal.

I was eleven years old when my father once again took up piloting in the Bristol Channel. In his younger days he had been a Bristol Channel Sailing pilot. I was often during the school holidays taken to spend time with him on board the pilot's berth 'Berkeley Castle' or the 'Alaska'. These were two cutters with their masts and sails removed, converted into houseboats and moored in the drain at Portishead. There was also a similar pilot cutter there named the 'Veritas'. She was built on the same lines as the 'Berkeley Castle' and 'Alaska' but she was two feet shorter.

Soon we moved from Gloucester to Sharpness and I was to become fascinated with all aspects of the river from then on. I would love to go on to the dock at tide time and watch the vessels as they docked. In those days there were innumerable oil carrying craft. The three different carrying companies on the river were: The Severn Carrying Company, The Regent Oil Company and John Harkers of Nottingley. There were also many general cargo carrying craft using the port, which included schooners, topsail schooners, and vessels up to approximately 10,000 tons; all taking timber and grain into Sharpness docks. It was a very busy port and at tide time the lock and the basin were always full of craft. It was only at special holiday times such as Christmas that things were more peaceful.

At night, I would watch the traffic on the river. I would see the petrol carriers, recognisable by the red light on their masts denoting inflammable or explosive cargo on board. There were craft with logs bound for Morelands of Gloucester to make Englands Glory matches; and many other kinds of cargo. No wonder I became fascinated with the river and all its aspects.

My father was born in a bungalow situated on the bank dividing the Sharpness canal and the river Severn, just North of the ill fated Severn Railway bridge (this bridge was later blown up by tankers in collision). My grandfather was the first engineer to operate the opening section of the Severn Railway Bridge across the canal, necessary to let through the large and high masted vessels. His name was Edward Lane, known locally as Teddy Lane. My father was his youngest son, Albert Lane. As a boy, I remember coming down the canal, boarding the passenger boats the 'Lapwing' or the 'Wave' at Llanthony Bridge Gloucester, and getting off at the Severn Railway Bridge, Sharpness. I would then run up the bank to Granny's bungalow. Although my grandfather worked for the railway, his job was directly related to the movement of shipping on the river and canal. My father's working life was all in shipping and most of it on the Severn. Myself and my two younger brothers naturally became river men, although my brothers did not as I, continue working the river. You could say that knowledge of the river Severn flows within the veins of the Lane family. I record these memories for everyone to know of the life and how we used to live and work aboard the Severn tankers and how we navigated the river.

My earliest voyage with my parents at Fowey. 'S.S. Seaforth'.

The Bristol Channel pilot cutter 'Veritas'.

'S.S. Seaforth'.

'S.S.Calcaria' Owned by Smith's of Bristol.

Chapter Two

The Small Tankers

Many men were engaged in life on the River Severn. They used to study the river, its changes of the seasons and the changes of the years. I was one of these men. I would not have missed for the world the comradeship of those unique people known as the Severn Tanker men.

The Severn tankers were nicknamed 'Severn Submarines' by the men because they sat so low in the water when fully laden. Their free board was between 6" to 12" and all that was visible from a distance was the mast and wheelhouse. Later, the more modern craft that started to emerge in the fifties, were a little different; the after end was built up, giving about 3ft from loaded water line, to deck level. The lower deck remained the same, at six to twelve inches from the water line. The lifeboat was athwart ships on the foredeck, there was not much freeboard. Being tankers, the water that came on board in bad weather when all hatches were battened down, quickly ran off again. In the old vessels, the accommodation was forward, consisting of one small cabin, which had three bunks, plus two seats that could be used as bunks if need be, a table and a two seater stool; very cramped. There was a locker for food, and an electric cooker, an electric kettle and two radiators that ran off a small generating set.

The engineless dumb barges would also when loaded be very low in the water, making them raft like in appearance. At any sign of the slightest heavy weather, with just about eight inches freeboard, everything had to be lashed down. With a heavy cargo the water washed the deck amidships. The fore-end had a bosun's store and toilet room, the after cabin was for two to four persons. The heating consisted of an Aladin paraffin cooker-come heating stove. This was inadequate for the job, due to the metal gauze safety covers on the heating top. This was put there to shield the naked flame against gasses. It took a good hour to boil a kettle, so against all safety regulations the two gauzes were taken off and a steel rowlock was put on top of the funnel instead. Most of our food was fried as this was the most practical way of serving it hot and anyway, we could only put one utensil on the stove at a time. The cabins were very spartan; the bare bunks and seats were bolted to the ship's ribs and the steelwork was also bare, making it extremely hot in summer and freezing cold in winter. It was always said that if you could endure the winter, the summer came easy. Many men came and went throughout the winter. The turnover of crew in those days was very high.

In 1946 I started work for the Regent Oil Company, which was attached to the Petroleum Board. Our trips always started from Avonmouth, and in the nineteen-fifties two other craft, which had been added to our fleet, used to run down to Cardiff and Swansea. This was very different to river tanking as they were going seaward, but they also ran up to Stourport-on-Severn so must be included as part of the river run. I was the Engineer on the Regent Robin at one stage. I have also been aboard them in the capacity of Master, but even with extra engine power, they were no different from the other craft in size. Their engines were much larger than the other vessels so they could not carry as much cargo.

When the new craft started to appear in the fifties, they came in pairs, the 'Regent Robin', and 'Regent Wren'; the 'Regent Lark' and 'Regent Linnett'; and the 'Regent Swift' and 'Regent Swallow'. These six vessels did not have dumb barges to tow, as by this time faster craft were needed. Accommodation aboard these craft was very comfortable. The Master's cabin, mess room and crew quarters, were all self contained. During the time I worked on board these craft, the Company issued you with two blankets and a mattress for the bunk, everything else you supplied yourself. At first we had a straw mattress, known to us as 'the donkey's breakfast'. Then when foam rubber came into being, we were issued foam rubber mattresses for the bunks, and still just the two blankets. In winter we had to use overcoats, plus our own blankets, sheets and pillows to keep warm. In extreme cold we sometimes left the paraffin heaters alight on the dumb barges, and on the motor craft, the Rattler (as the generating engine was affectionately known) was left running all night. In summer if it was hot, we used to haul our mattresses on deck and sleep beneath the stars. Very healthy, so it was said. Until there was an unexpected thunder storm. Then what fun we had trying to rush back down to the cabin with all our bedding before it got wet. You can imagine the scene. A sudden storm, two or three men sleeping on deck, and only one small hatchway. Bedclothes and mattresses were thrown down the companion way closely followed the crew. Then came the business of sorting out whose bedding was whose before retiring; hilarious at the best of times.

Chapter Three

Living on Board

Living on board the small craft was certainly an education. It taught many a young boy to look after himself properly. To keep clean and tidy, to buy food and manage with money (most had to send money home), and still have enough left to buy personal things. In some respects he had to keep two homes; it was harder for the married men who had families to support as well.

From the time a boy came on board until he was a man, hard work was the order of the day. As a boy, he had certain jobs to do besides looking after the living quarters. Sometimes in cleaning the quarters he had help from other members of the crew, if work on deck had been completed. He had to strip the cabin, or cabins (the earlier vessels only had one cabin, large enough for four to sleep). In the later craft there were three cabins; the Masters, the crew's and the mess room. He had to clean and scrub these out from top to bottom twice a week.Usually this was on the return journey of our trips, so that everything was spotless and clean ready for our return after we had spent a few hours at home. The mats (providing the weather was dry) were thrown out on deck, swept, then scrubbed, The steps of the companion way had to be scrubbed white or they were considered unclean. All the pots and pans were washed up, cleaned and put away, the kettle had to be polished, the cooking stove cleaned, and lastly the brass in the cabin had to be cleaned and shined. Everything was then 'Ship-shape and Bristol fashion', as they say.

Each man was responsible for his own bedding, so after we had got under way every member of the crew from the Master down, had to make his bunk whenever he could get below. Then it would be clear for the deck boy to do his chores. In such confined living space, cleanliness was next to Godliness. In the later craft, which had three cabins, the deck hand would help the boy because the work was too much for him to do alone. Usually he had to clean the wheelhouse as well. That meant while we were loading them he would clean all the brass in and

One of the new small tankers on her maiden voyage, the 'M.V. Regent Robin'.

One of the larger tankers that ran to Worcester, the 'M.V. Darleydale'.

around the wheelhouse. If we had been out in heavy weather, the brasswork would become green from the effects of salt water. It took a lot of cleaning. Finally the duck boards were lifted, scrubbed and refitted, then the wooden deck head over the accommodation deck would also be scrubbed clean and white. We had a special powder to shake and scrub with, and long handled deck scrubbers. Considering the amount of oil that was walked through, believe me it was very hard work. The wheelhouse windows had to be as clean as a new pin or the skipper came down on one very hard.

From early spring and during the summer months there was the never ending job of chipping and wire brushing rust from the pipe lines, decks, and staunchions, and then red leading them. Once this had been done, they had to be painted from stem to stern until they were smart, clean and tidy. When chipping, we had to be aware of the cargo we were carrying. If our load was spirit, i.e., motor petrol (for we carried many grades of this), or something with a very high flashpoint, we could not safely chip the rust away in case it created sparks. So instead, a scraper and a wire brush had to be used. This involved hours and hours of work cleaning off rust. At the end of the day these river tankers were a credit to their Masters and crews. We always kept some tar brushes in the bosun's store to put a coat of tar on the hull when empty, above the 'empty' water line. We used to moor against a low wall or something similar and do the hull around, then paint the draft marks back in, to finish the job.

Whenever we were on board, the tea pot was never cold. We had our cuppa on average about every two hours. Although I have now been ashore for eleven years, my wife tells me I have not lost my habit of regular tea drinking!

All the years I worked on the tankers we always had a cooked meal at mid-day. This would be on the upward journey from Sharpness or Gloucester to Stourport. It was always a full three course meal including a sweet to follow. At these times I was always grateful to have learnt as much as I possibly could about cooking. Whatever was being cooked, everyone mucked in. One had to remember that all the other routine jobs on board had still to be done. A new boy was always taught the rudiments of cooking. Even now nothing deters me from cooking at home whenever I get the chance.

I remember on one occasion we had eaten a good cooked meal at Avonmouth and were bound for Sharpness, but had no time to wash up then as we had to stand to for sailing. By the time we had tidied everything on deck we were up the channel near the Lyde at Beachley. The boy then went below to wash up. I decided to take a short cut across the sands thinking I had just the right depth of water. I had miscalculated and we came to a sudden stop. We were aground on a sand bank. The tide piled on one side and she started to list over. The boy was by this time down in the mess room washing up with the washing bowl that was sitting at the end of the table. The bowl began to move and slowly slide away from him. He panicked and shot up to the deck as white as a sheet. We assured him that everything was all right as the tide was still rising. After a short while she lifted and we were on our way again, but it was amusing to see the look on the boy's face as he bolted from out of the companion way hatch.

Chapter Four

My First Position

In 1940, when I was 16 years old, I started aboard the 'Regent Queen'. In those days the craft operated in pairs, a motor craft and a 'dumb' craft. In the Regent Oil Company the ladies always came first. The 'Queen' was the motor and was followed by the 'King', the other four craft with the company were the 'Jill' and 'Jack' and the 'Lady' and 'Lord'.

Before my time on the river, there was an oil storage depot at Sharpness, owned and operated by the then Power Petrol Company. There were not many craft that ran from there up the river to Gloucester in those days. These first craft to do so were all the engineless dumb barges; they were nicknamed by the men the Black Bats and the Cowmouths. The 'Severn Pioneer' and the 'Severn Venturer' were the Black Bats, and the 'Severn Commerce' and 'Severn Conveyer' were the Cowmouths. These craft would load at Sharpness, carry up the canal to Gloucester, then lock back out into the river for Worcester and Stourport-on-Severn. They were towed up the canal by large sea tugs, and then on by the Severn and Canal Carrying Company tugs. These tugs were based at Gloucester Quay, so they were always on station ready to tow the barges plus general cargo craft to their destination.

After this, the amount of craft started to increase as the depots up and down the river began to grow. During the war years the number of craft working on the Severn was great. At the height of this period, there were four depots at Stourport, and one at Worcester, War Ministry depots at other places on the river, and five at Gloucester. The War Ministry ones were underground. Being war time, these craft were vital to keep the depots full of the grades of oil. During the war, the oil trade was controlled by the Petroleum Board.

Towards the end of the war, the oil depots were gradually closed down and this marked the beginning of the decline of the

Smoking was allowed on board the tankers but only in the cabin, wheelhouse, and on the after-deck. Not at anytime when loading and discharging.

Towing close up with crossed tow ropes. The 'Regent Jill' with the 'Regent Jack' in the canal at Gloucester Docks.

river traffic. For many years the Regent Oil Company was the only company to operate their craft on the Severn and was known originally as the Trinidad Leasehold Ltd.; until they were taken over.

I was apprenticed to the Regent vessels to learn the river and eventually to become a Master if I could pass the Company exams and showed the right abilities. I had a good teacher in my father. When I was off duty, I used to go out with him and with Captain Whittington the Harbour Master, on surveys of the river outside Sharpness. The channel pilots also taught me a lot, I was taught to respect the river, this was drummed into me over the years so that I would remember how treacherous the river could be. This stood me in good stead. The cardinal rule to me was, 'Treat Sabrina with respect and she will do the same for you, but abuse her and she will certainly abuse you'.

Chapter Five

How the River was worked

The second vessel I served on was the 'Regent Jill', the master was Captain Ernest Lundergard whom I served for some years. My wages in those days were five shillings per week, in addition we were paid a little extra for any trips we did within that week. I would also be paid two shillings and sixpence for working on a Sunday. So all told, I was well paid. There was also a payment of three shillings and sixpence danger money, as we were prime targets for the enemy! Then, German planes were sowing mines and strafing any craft they spotted in the river and Bristol Channel. They made things very uncomfortable for us.

Our life was hard; the living accommodation sparse. The wheelhouse had no doors, only a canvas dodger each side to keep out any bad weather. Doors were eventually fitted but this was many years later. The carrying capacity of these craft was approximately 150 tons, and the dumb barges were 180 tons. There were other craft owned by different firms that were larger than these, but they were limited to Worcester. They could carry somewhere in the region of 250 to 300 tons. I spent my time with the Regent Oil Company from 1940 until they finished in the middle sixties. The Regent craft had 140hp marine diesels, made by Ruston and Hornsby. This enabled the men to change from craft to craft and still be familiar with the propelling equipment and the engine rooms.

The trip started at Avonmouth, our loading point, and headed for Sharpness. We locked into the canal, then back into the river at Gloucester and up to Stourport-on-Severn in Worcestershire. Then we would head back once more to Gloucester, into the canal, and out on the tide at Sharpness to sail back to Avonmouth again. This was a round trip of approximately three days. We would do this twice a week, and we were paid by the trip. If we wanted to earn more money, we would work longer hours by putting an extra trip into one week. This extra trip would run into the following week, so we had to sail as fast as we could, working all hours of the day and night to make sure we had enough time to make our normal two trips in the coming week. If we broke down and went alongside the wall, we were not paid trip money, just our basic wage. Working on a Sunday would boost our wages a little more.

By other standards on shore, our wages were very good, but the hours were abnormal. For instance, we would leave Sharpness on the tide at three o'clock in the morning for Avonmouth, load there, and when we returned to Sharpness that following night, it was around five or six o'clock in the evening before we had finished. In that one day we would have worked fourteen to fifteen hours. The following morning we would be away from Sharpness about five o'clock to go to Stourport and discharge our cargo and then head back to Worcester to moor up. By then it was about eight or nine o'clock at night and made a fifteen or sixteen hour working day. Next morning we were away at five o'clock again, to arrive at Sharpness at around two p.m., a nine hour day, making a long three day trip. We could then have a few hours off to go home. I lived at Sharpness in those days. Next day we had to turn out again for the tide, so we didn't have much time spare, especially as it was war time. We had to keep going, day in and day out.

There was no room for mistakes. Everything was done with common sense and good judgement. To dock at Sharpness fully loaded was a very tricky business, especially if there was a big tide. It was as much as we could do to hold the craft in the flow of the tide. We would come up the river, arrive off Berkeley Pill and then swing between either the Berkeley Power Station and Sharpness, or the Berkeley Pill and Sharpness (There is a navigation light here termed the swinging light). Then we would head in towards the shore. In the run of a 30ft tide. Our speed was only about six knots, or about four knots if we were towing. We then dropped with the tide, or held close to the shore to wait and watch for the signal for us to dock into Sharpness. The signal was hanging on the yard arm, or if it was after dark, a light shone on the signal mast. When we saw the signal to dock, we had to pull out into the tide and gently drop back. We would then skim the South Pier with our bow, and pull into the slack waters behind the Pier. At the same time we would let the dumb barge come behind to drop in on our starboard quarter. Then we would give the engines everything we had to pull into Sharpness. We then skimmed the South Pier with our bow, we were never more than a foot from it. At night the mast head light lit the pier and that was the only way we could judge our distance from it. If we made a mistake, we didn't have a second chance, the only thing we could do in those circumstances was to drop behind the North Pier, patiently wait for the tide to ease, and then dock.

We used to run the river in low water, at high tide and at low tide. Of course, we had to know exactly where we could safely go according to the tide at the time. Before the Power Stations Oldbury and Berkeley were there, and before the Severn Bridge was built; on a large or high tide we could run our tide from Sharpness by going down inshore. We ran close to the shore at Fishing House, Shepperdine, Oldbury, Aust, Pilning and Avonmouth. If we were short of time, it helped to know these short cuts. If we left Avonmouth late on the upward run, we knew where we could go to save time. If we were running for Sharpness from Avonmouth and if the tide was high with enough water, we could go straight across between the English Stones and the New Passage, and across to the Lyde. Then we would sail to Inward Rocks and on up to the Gusker Rocks across the river between Shepperdine Sands and Lydney Sands to Berkeley Power Station or Berkeley Pill and then finally into Sharpness. Also if there was enough water, we could run up to Lydney from the Gusker Rocks. We went this way to Sharpness, past Lydney Docks, across the river and straight into Sharpness Docks. Of course, it meant you had to know the tricks of the river because of the sand banks and the depth of the water that you had to play with. You only had limited time to dock at Sharpness because any vessels in the Basin had to be locked in after high tide to enter Sharpness Canal. We were always chasing time and tide, which waits for no man.

Chapter Six

Tricks, Marks and Incidents

Apart from my father, other men who taught me were the Harbour Master of Sharpness, and old Percy Palmer the Light Keeper at Shepperdine. I was taught to observe the four tall chimneys on the Power Station at Portishead (which have since been demolished). If we wanted to run down the south shore from Northwick Buoy just below Aust, we could line up two of these chimneys one behind the other, and run down the Channel on that side of the river to Avonmouth. This saved time against going down from the Chapel Rock to Charston Rock and across Kingroad to Avonmouth. Another mark was to know how much water was in Kingroad up to the Lyde. We knew that the Bedwin Sands (off Portishead); the Bull Rock at the approximate centre of the Channel off Pilning; and the Lyde Rock, went under water at three hours to High Water Sharpness time, and gave about 30 feet of water in Kingroad.

The next marks were the rungs on the Lyde Light. The bottom three were eight feet apart and the top two ten feet. When the water was half way up to the second rung, there was twelve feet of water on the rock. This meant you had just eight feet across the Shepperdine Sands from the Gusker Rocks to Berkeley Pill, or if it was tight, to Hayward buoy off Fishing House. If the water was up to the third rung, you had water up the Lydney shore and across to Sharpness. However, by this time you were running very late on tide, so you had to use this side to get more tide run.

We had learnt that the tide still flowed up the Lydney shore even when it had stopped flowing on the Sharpness side, which gave a better chance of docking. Sometimes a marker buoy was taken off station for service. Then you needed to know the other marks for navigating the river. For instance, when Hayward buoy was off station, all you had to do was to look (in the daytime) at Lydney church spire. When it went into the cleft of the two hills behind it, you were passing Hayward Rock. The Bull Perch off Berkeley Pill had two foot markers upon it, and read correctly, it would tell you how much tide had flowed or ebbed and what water was on Sharpness outer sill. If you knew this, it told you what water you had up through the Bull Channel. Once, Captain Rowles (the author of the book 'Sharpness, the Country Port') had a yacht owner on board his craft for a river trip. As I was Master of the 'Regent Jill' then, I was edging my way through this channel and he was half an hour behind me. He said to his passenger, 'Do you realise that the "Regent Jill" going up through the channel has only about six inches of water under her? That is what is called working the river very fine.' When I docked at Sharpness he asked me if it was true what the Captain had told him. I said that it was, and that I did know what clearance I had underneath my craft.

There have been many collisions and tragedies on the river. The first tanker tragedy with loss of life, was when I was about twelve years old. The 'Severn Traveller', the 'Severn Carrier I' and the 'Severn Venturer' a dumb barge were off from Sharpness early, on a very high tide. There were eight men on board the three craft. The 'Severn Carrier I' broke down; the 'Severn Traveller' tried to rescue her but was carried up river by the strong tide, desperately trying to pull the other two inshore, but they touched the sand banks and were rolled over and over. Five of the eight men lost their lives.

One very tragic accident involved a vessel called the 'B.P. Explorer', this was on the evening of February 16th, 1961. I was not out in the river that night, but I have spoken to Masters of vessels that were, and we have formed our own conclusions.

I understand it was a clear night, with no fog and visibility very good. Now, whether this has any bearing on what happened I really don't know, but from the day that vessel came into service on her maiden voyage, it seemed as though she was jinxed, for she was often in trouble and frequently in dry dock or the repair yards.

On that particular night that jinx must have worked overtime for the three men and two boys of her crew were lost.

It seems that the Explorer had left Swansea with approximately 450 tons of motor spirit bound for Worcester. She was up and past Avonmouth and crossing the Kingroad before the other vessels were locked out of Avonmouth and bound for Sharpness so she was very early on tide. Also she was most probably trying to be early enough to be in first lock at Sharpness. Ahead of her travelling up the channel was another craft drawing less water and much smaller than the 'B.P. Explorer' and there were craft coming up the channel behind her. She was seen to go up the Slimeroad channel by the Masters of other craft, they were watching her navigation lights so knew just where she was. Sometimes you could miss a vessel out there because of the enormous amount of shore lights twinkling all around, but provided you knew what you were looking for you could pick them up again after a few minutes.

The 'Explorer' was seen to turn to starboard at Inward Rocks to make passage across to Shepperdine. Now it was a very high and very strong tide, probably running about 13 knots. In these conditions all Masters had to cross this part of the channel very carefully and in a somewhat crab like fashion. I personally have been up very early and have actually been heading for Aust and used the tide to cross to Shepperdine. Here, once behind the rocks at Oldbury it took the power out of the tide so it was a bit easier to handle your vessel.

If this was her masters intention and we *do* know he was early on tide, he probably caught his keel on Shepperdine sands, and the relentless power of the tide flow just rolled his craft over and over. If he had been a bit later, there would have been enough water to carry him safely across the river. As it was, the crew would have had no chance of escape.

Later, when she was missed, one of the skippers said that when he was waiting to dock into Sharpness he thought he saw a hulk float up by in the middle of the river. She was upside down so this was no doubt the 'Explorer'. She drifted up and down the river for several tides finally coming to rest at the village of Awre on the Forest of Dean side of the river. No bodies were found in the engine room or accommodation. They must have been lost in the river somewhere.

When she was eventually salvaged she was taken to dry dock and rebuilt. Once rebuilt she was renamed the 'B.P. Driver'. However, the jinx was not finished with her because, in November the following year she ran ashore at the Nash Point and was so badly damaged she was cut up and scrapped.

Once, when the 'Regent Queen' and 'Regent King' were empty and bound for Avonmouth from Sharpness, the motor craft was towing inshore to get out of the hard tide. She went aground on the breakwater north of Fishing House. The 'Queen' was drawing about 5ft 6in of water and the dumb barge only 2ft. The dumb barge shot off to port, the tow rope parted and she ran ashore. The motor craft tried to get off the breakwater but the tide turned, and both vessels stuck. The tide receded, and the next tide was about 2 ft less in height so the motor craft managed to get off the breakwater, but the dumb barge was so far up on the shore she could not be removed until many days later on the next high spring tides, and then she had virtually to be re-launched.

An amusing incident happened at the time. The first night the 'Regent King' was up on the shore, some cows from a farm close by came down to graze. They spotted the vessel and started rubbing themselves against her sides, this woke and startled the crew. In the darkness they were afraid to go up on deck to see what was going on. Next morning they summoned up courage to go up on deck but by then the cows had gone away. They carried their bikes, which they had on board, up to the road, and made for home as fast as they could. They didn't spend another night on board, all the time she was there.

Sometimes, on days when the river and channel were mirror calm, upon leaving Sharpness Light Ship for Avonmouth, we would sail out and ease the craft down to moor alongside one another. In this fashion we would traverse the river from Sharpness to Avonmouth. I have been in company this way when three motor vessels have moored alongside each other, with fenders put between them, their tow craft have done the same; and we have gone to Avonmouth in this way. This meant that just one man was steering all six vessels. The centre leading vessel was the one we navigated from. When we arrived off Avonmouth we would part company, take our dumb craft alongside and then dock into Avonmouth.

Chapter Seven

Aspects of the work in the Channel and above Gloucester

Severn Tankers were designed for maximum carrying capacity, but had to fit the Bevere, Holt and Lincombe locks above Worcester. To get the dumb craft into the locks when they were loaded, we had to tow them in with a tow rope over the centre of the top gate. When they were in, we then had to pull the rudders right up against the stern end, to enable the lock gate to be shut. When they were lifted up in the lock, the top gates were opened and the motor craft started to tow them out. The rudder then was released and put back into position for steering. This was how tight it was in the locks. Once the motor was in the lock, the gates were shut ready to lift them up. The motor was put into 'astern' to keep them from going under the beams of the lock gates and lifting them off their pivot. On the dumb barge the crew would put pieces of timber on their bows and hold them there so that the bow slid up these and not catch under the lock beams. Otherwise it lifted a gate off and a repair crew and diver would have to come from Worcester andthe river traffic was stopped until it was repaired.

During the war years, we were given our orders and we had to sail in fog, wind or whatever weather, to ensure our cargoes got through. Some of the dumps or tanks we discharged at were built underground so they could not be seen from the air. Some of our cargoes were 230, 200, 150 octane rated, some were so light a fuel that craft appeared only half loaded when actually, it was completely full up. The flashpoint of these cargoes was very high, so we had to be extra careful in the handling of them. As jet engines appeared on the scene, our cargoes changed to A.T.F. (Aircraft Turbine Fuel).

The port of Sharpness in those days, was a hive of activity. I have seen a tug leave Sharpness for Gloucester at 5 a.m. with as many as eighteen dumb barges in tow, some with oil and others with general cargo. They would not reach Gloucester before about eight o'clock at night. In those days, they were steam tugs. With a tow of that amount, they would get up perhaps to Frampton, which is about half way up the canal, stop to clean the boiler tubes out and then carry on to Gloucester.

When I started work on board the tankers, I had to go from deck boy, deck hand, dumb barge hand, dumb barge master, engineer of motor craft, mate, then eventually skipper. By doing this, I was taught all aspects of the work, and then as Master I had to make my own decisions. I was taught to splice, tie knots and everything appertaining to seamanship. I remember making stern fenders with old rope slung between davits on board, and working on them for days on end, to replace the ones that were worn out. In the winter the hard frost made the tow ropes like a bar of ice. When we stopped towing we had to pull the ropes in by hand and the ice made our hands hurt badly. If the ropes were frozen, and the motor set them up too hard, they would snap and that meant another splicing job. We always used inlaid manila, which was a hell of a job to splice. Our company never used wire and springs, but one of the other companies did. I have seen wire that has been set up too fast and too hard, snap and cut a man's legs off. They were very dangerous.

If we sailed in rough weather and tried to get around Beachley Head, and the wind proved too bad, we had to go back into Slimeroad and lie on the mud flats under the navigation lights on shore. That was one of the safe places in fog or rough weather. We didn't have many quiet moments, the job had to be done and we did it, especially during the war years. We snatched a few hours sleep whenever we could. We became very tired and sometimes fell asleep standing up. This happened once when a skipper nodded off going down past Charston Rock, and someone happened eventually to go up on deck and found they were nearly at the Denny Island about four miles downstream. They had to wake up the skipper and bring her back round for Avonmouth.

Chapter Eight

Getting the best out of Sabrina and Times and Courses

On one side of the Severn tide line, the water ran faster than the other, this was where the tide ran say, close to a sand bank or rocks. We had to have the nerve to get near the tide line, the nearer we got the faster the tide ran, so the faster our vessel moved through the water.

There have been some amusing incidents through these runs of tide. I remember once when we turned up river at Charston. The nearer we got to it before turning, the faster we moved. Owing to the fact there was a split in the tide, some water going up the River Wye, the other up past Chapel Rock, the tide run stopped into slow water and our craft was apt to dive. I saw two such vessels bury themselves there, one of them was the 'Severn Venturer'. Her fore end stores hatch and the cabin hatch to the aft, were open. When she hit the dead water she dived and the open compartments filled with water. The skipper stood at the wheel, up to his waist in water. The other craft was the 'Severn Carrier', she did exactly the same. The skipper and mate saw what was about to happen, so they rushed out of the wheelhouse onto to the top of the tank lids. Both vessels were dumb barges, but if the motor craft had eased its pulling speed back, it would not have happened. They could speed up again, go in toward the Wye, and the run of tide would start again towards the Chapel Rock. Here again strong nerves were needed to navigate close in the run of the tide, then you were off at speed.

During the summer in daylight tides, we used to have a book, pen, and clock in the wheelhouse taking times and courses. We wrote down the height of the tide, the weather conditions, the speed or r.p.m. of the engine and whether we were towing or not. We used to take these to be used during foggy weather, or if we were caught out in the river in fog. They were taken both ways on the river, and were invaluable to us. The river could be so dangerous, you had to keep them on board and up to date always. To give you some idea, times and courses taken from Sharpness on the down run, were started abreast of the south pier. You set your bow on to Berkeley Pill navigation lights, took the time and course, then steered until the next set of lights marking when the deep water channel came into line, which in this case was Fishing House. You then turned on to these, took the time and your new course, wrote it down, then carried on until you turned to your next deep water channel course. Then you took times and course again and so on, to Avonmouth.

I remember once, a certain crew had the silly habit of putting the ship's cabin and hatch keys in the binnacle. Of course, because they contained iron they drew the magnetic compass. They sailed from Sharpness this particular night, it was a very dirty fog, with visibility right down. They set their course according to their book, and were puzzled when they found themselves aground under the cliffs at Lydney. Another craft had sailed out of Lydney and the Master put his look out up forward and ran his times and courses. After some time he asked his look out if he could see anything. His look out turned and said 'Aye Cap'n, some sheep under our bow'. It seems they had crossed the river and were aground on the entrance of Sanigar Pill.

Chapter Nine

The Engineer's Life

As engineers, we had to keep our engine rooms clean and tidy, we would repaint when needed and also look after the engine oil pressures, fuel oil, time and log sheets, daily running sheets and everything appertaining to the engine room. When I took over, the engineers position on board 'Regent Robin', I had to wash down and paint the engine room completely, which took me some months. I had just finished, when a Lloyds insurance surveyor arrived on board to make his regular inspection. He was just about to put his overalls on in the office on shore, when he was told by the ship's husband (who looks after ship's business on shore), he would not need them because it was very clean on board this craft. How flattered and elated I felt on hearing of this. I knew my hard work had not gone unnoticed.

Another craft I served as engineer on, had side valve engines, that were old and worn. The valves were in their cases and could consequently change without a decoke, or the head being removed. One day we had an exhaust valve stuck. I had a very limited time to change it, so I started to strip it ready for removal. Well, right opposite in the engine room was a lavatory that had outside on its door a framed plaque showing the key colours of the pipe layout such as water, fuel and oil. We tried all ways of getting this valve out. The only way I could see to do it was to connect it up loosely, take the fuel off the piston cylinder, turn the air on to it and see if it would loosen that way. Before I could cut the fuel off, the skipper, impatient in case we missed the tide, put the air through the engine, making the cylinder fire. It shot the encased valve like a bullet across the engine room, scored a bullseye in the centre of the plaque, and continued on through the door panel to finally complete its journey in the lavatory pan, smashing it. The holding bolts were stripped so we could not sail on that tide. Instead we then had to change the cylinder head. Eventually, I began to see the funny side of the incident. I still have a chuckle at it today.

We had all sorts of trouble with deck engines and cargo pumps, including salt water corrosion from heavy weather, and ice from freezing weather. These engines were from 25 h.p. upwards and had to be started by hand in a confined space where there was hardly any room to swing the handle. The small engines from 15 h.p. upwards in the engine room were the same. They had to generate the electricity for cooking and also to pump compressed air to start the main engines. They always had to be in perfect running order. The deck engine also had two jobs. It was connected to the cargo pump, which in turn had to pump cargo and ballast water in or out of the hold as required.

In the 1950's John Harkes introduced much larger craft for the Worcester run. These then started to bypass Avonmouth and run on down channel to Swansea, as the Llandarcy Refinery was opened then. During the period of the larger craft sailing to Worcester, Shell and B.P. brought out some tankers to join in this work, run and crewed by J. Harker men, these craft had Schnieder Gear, a revolutionary propelling and steering equipment. However, this innovation proved to be a mistake in the River Severn above Gloucester, as the silt, mud, sand and sunken tree trunks soon caused unrepairable damage.

Chapter Ten

Avonmouth, Our Loading Point

It was at Avonmouth that Captain Morgan and Captain Lunderguard made sure that I, as a boy, read and learned the Ports of Bristol Authority Byelaws. These byelaws applied to every kind of craft using the P.B.A. Dock, whatever its size or cargo. As Master of a vessel you could be taken to court for contravening the Byelaws and as I will describe later, I very nearly was.

We used to dock at Avonmouth light, have the dumb barge alongside on crossed ropes, knock the dogs out of the dumb barge rudder so that it was free, then go up the dock to load. If these dogs or catches were not knocked out of the steering gear, the dumb barge could not be handled alongside. Across the entrance to the oil dock, there was a powered oil boom. It was always in place, except to let tankers or other vessels in and out for bunkering. As we entered the lock from the seaward side, the harbour watchman on duty used to take our names and collect our customs forms. He then gave us our berth number, and we locked up and then proceeded to our berths. This routine worked admirably for all the years I worked on board tankers. Once all the tankers were in the oil dock, the boom was closed until the next tide. This was done to safeguard all the other vessels in case of fire. It was opened by arrangement if we were going out into the main dock between tides, such as for a compass check or to go to the dry dock for minor repairs.

During the war years, several alarming events occurred at Avonmouth. One night, we arrived in Avonmouth entrance aboard the 'Regent King' and 'Regent Queen' during an enemy air raid alert. We had the dumb barge alongside and moored on the pier while waiting to enter the docks. Because of the alert, the docks were closed to shipping. Suddenly, on shore, a bomb hit a storage tank holding some two hundred tons of paraffin. It caught fire and lit up the whole of Avonmouth Dock as if it were daylight. We were on deck and the Captain decided to run to a safer anchorage in Walton Bay down the coast. So we slipped our moorings, dropped the dumb barge onto a large tow rope and started to run for it. We had not thought that we could be clearly seen in the light from the blaze. Sure enough, we were spotted by an enemy aircraft and bombs were dropped. As we were looking out of the rear wheelhouse windows, we saw the bombs exploding in the water, heading nearer. The last one landed alongside the dumb barge. I swear that we could see right underneath her as she left the water by at least two feet.

Another evening, we loaded and moored close to the oil boom. We were used to air raids by now, but were unprepared for a sudden terrific explosion. We all dashed up on deck, to be told by a soldier on shore that a bomb had dropped the other side of the oil boom, within 100 yards of us. The bomb was approximately 500 pounds.

Once, we were loading at 'number 5' oil berth under the bow of a large sea-going tanker, that had a hole in the starboard side of the fore peak, about three feet in diameter. When we had docked in the early hours, we had not noticed the hole until a mobile crane with some navy men and dry dock workers arrived and, with acetylene equipment cut the hole larger. Bearing in mind we were loading oil or petrol, it began to get a bit scary to say the least. When the hole was big enough they drew the hook of the crane into it with rope and other lashings. After a while the crane driver was told to haul, then out of the ship's forepeak appeared a live torpedo. It was pulled clear and was there, swinging in the breeze.

When I remember what we used to do to get loaded in time for the tide in my early years at Avonmouth, it was a wonder to me that we did not blow ourselves up, without the German airforce doing it for us. But it was all part of the war effort. For instance our loading pipes came in all sizes, four inch, eight inch and even ten inch pipes. In those days we used very heavy iron ended pipes, made with canvas, rubber and stripped with thick steel wire, which had very little bend in them. Today's pipes are made with light alloy ends and a very light composite rubber with some sort of plastic composition. We could hardly bend the old pipes and it was all hands to the fore to get them connected to the shore delivery line, and to the ship. We used to connect two or three together, sometimes more, and run them across other craft, putting old tyres, coils of rope, old fenders – anything we could to stop them causing sparks. Today, this is not, *definitely not*, allowed. The loading was always done by the mate. We used to load to a specific draft to get over the Lincombe Sill at Stourport-on-Severn, the furthest port on this river, if we were bound for that depot. For any other destination we could fill the craft up to the ullage bars in the tank lids. Loading to these ullage boards was very precise. Before the cargo came aboard, the lid top had to be opened, and the gauze for the release of gases as the tanks filled, in place. The average tank lid was approximately 4ft x 2ft with the porthole shaped top set into it. The large lid, was bolted down with ten large bolts. The porthole type one for loading and discharging was hinged one side and had a screw type catch for the Customs seal. This was because all cargoes were still under bond. Customs duty had not been paid, so it had to be sealed before leaving the berth. It was necessary for the lid on the tanks to be open when loading. I remember once when one lid was forgotten. The build up of pressure from the cargo coming on board blew the whole lid off, stripping the holding bolts as it did so. The lid sailed through the air for about a quarter of a mile. It went flying over the jetty, the pipe ground, the road, the large Shell depot and landed on the fore-shore the other side.

It was here at Avonmouth that young men joining tankers were initiated into tanking life, and as there were always twenty or thirty craft in the oil dock, it was an ideal place to learn. All the old hands would know just how to deal with any young man who was sent on board his craft to ask a peculiar question. One prank we played was to send them to the farthest vessel away from the one he worked upon, and to ask the master of that vessel if his Captain could borrow the key of the keelson. Of course, there was no such thing, but very often he was given a very heavy object to carry back to his vessel. When he arrived back, he was told that it was the wrong size, or wrong type, and told to take it back again. He would soon realise that he had been caught out. Usually after returning it to the vessel the skipper would drop him a clue he couldn't possibly miss. From then on he was on his guard against being caught out, and strangely enough he used to learn a lot better.

Another time, we were issued with clogs to try for loading and discharging on deck. To load we usually had to drop the safety stanchions and chains to get the pipe on board, to connect up for these operations. The clogs were supposed to be safe on board, because being wooden, they would not create sparks. What was overlooked was that as the wood soaked up oil, they became as slippery as ice. This being so, I saw a man slip while trying to help with the pipe. He fell over the side between some iron girders at the jetty, and into the dock. He was a very lucky man, he missed hitting any of the iron work, and just landed in the water, where we were quickly able to get him out. After this, we stopped using clogs. Even so, if in rain we wore sea boots and sou'westers, the seaboots had much the same effect as clogs, it was just as if there were a sheet ice on deck.

The byelaws were very strict. I remember on instance when the mate was loading my vessel, and I gave him instructions to fill the vessel to the ullage bars. As one tank came up, the speed of the cargo coming to the bar was very fast. As he shut the valve, some spirit splashed out of the inspection hole in the tank lid. Fortunately it did not go into the dock, which would have broken the law. Standing by the jetty was a P.B.A. policeman, who duly noted the incident. A few weeks later, I as Master was summoned to the Inspector of the P.B.A. Police Force. Luckily, as I had previously found out from the jetty hands and my crew for a full account of the incident. I was able to argue that as no spirit had gone into the dock, there was no case. The fine for this action if it had been proven was a maximum of £500! I was pleased I had learned my byelaws well, but there were many men who were not so lucky.

When sailing time came, there was always a rush at the dock to get into the lock first. If you could get out of Avonmouth and hit the tide off the pier, the other craft would have to move fast to reach Sharpness before you. If you could get to Sharpness and into the first lock there were definite advantages. You could finish an hour in front of second lock and two hours in front of third. I can remember the Avonmouth tug men keeping their vessels away from the lock at Avonmouth because they knew that the tanker men bound for Sharpness wanted a good run. To be able to get into the lock first, it was every man for himself. Fenders and crews were always at the ready and the bumping and boring that went on often caused tempers to flare, but it was taken in good humour afterwards. Sometimes the Harbour Master had quite a few deep sea-going ships to sail, so he would order us to be ready at four and a half hours to flow, instead of four hours. He would have the ship and its attending tugs in the lock, and would pack us all around it. Then he would lower the lock away, stop it at a certain height and wait for the tide to reach the same level. At this point the gates would be opened. The tankers would be ready with their engines revving flat out, then spill into the harbour like a pack of eager dogs let into a yard. We could coax more speed out of our engines if we got up to certain illegal tricks. On the Regents 'Jill', 'Lady' and 'Queen', it was possible to undo the engine governors so that the weights spread evenly to allow the engine more speed. On the newer engines, we always made sure that we had a few of the old eight sided threepenny pieces ready to place on the governor so that when the arm came over we could slip the coins onto the plunger. This would push it farther down and produce more speed.

Some of the other craft had 'Gardener' engines. These they improvised with a spring tied to the governor which pulled it back further, this also gave more revs and speed. One man did this, and later forgot to remove the spring. Whilst he was moored up for the weekend, the fitters came on board to give the engine an oil change. When they found the illegal spring they handed it into the fleet office. The Skipper was sent for. When he went into the office, the Manager of the Fleet was sat behind his desk swinging the offending article in his hand. The Skipper, seeing this, knew that he was in trouble. He decided to brazen it out, and said innocently 'I wondered where our garden gate spring had gone'. Well, the manager was so impressed by his cheek, he just told him to get out. He was lucky to get away with it. He certainly gave his engineer an earful when he got back on board for not removing that spring.

34

Waiting to lock in at Avonmouth.

Packed in the lock prior to sailing at Avonmouth.

Two light craft traversing the canal at Hardwicke. Note the old swing bridge.

Two vessels in the channel bound for Avonmouth and roped together.

Chapter Eleven

Sharpness and the Canal
to Gloucester Dock

In the early days the docks were always working to capacity. If we were not going on to Gloucester, we had to edge our way out of the main dock into the old dock, or the canal to moor up. We were not allowed to moor within the dock because of fire risks. If some of the craft had urgent cargoes, or if the crews wanted to carry on working they could travel on to Gloucester at night. This was possible because all the vessels were fitted with a pair of head lights fixed to the bow, one headlight to shine on the port bank and the other on the starboard bank. These were used extensively up to the time I finished, and were indispensable.

In those early days we had to book the time we wanted to go up the canal and we had to hire the passman. This was a man who earned his living by cycling on the canal tow path and opening and closing the bridges. If there was a fleet of craft, say fourteen or fifteen, there were two passmen. The canal bridges were in two halves and starting from Purton up the canal, or Hempstead down, the bridge was ordered for say, five in the morning and the passman would open the tow path side of the bridge. The resident bridgemen, who lived in a bungalow alongside each bridge, would open the other side, then in turn the tankers would go through. The other passman (if there were two of them) would ride his bicycle to the next bridge, open it, then ride on, the other passman following behind to close them when the last craft had gone through. If there was only one, or a pair of craft, one passman would do. Sometimes the amount of work was so great there were no passmen available. The deck boy was then put ashore and had to do the job riding along the canal bank, for this he would be paid extra. As a deck boy I had to do this frequently myself, and in those days the canal bank was not piled as it is now and was often subsiding into the canal.

The tow path sometimes went with it, leaving about six inches of path to ride on. This was hair raising at times, especially in the dark. Usually the resident bridgeman would warn you if the bank had gone, so you were aware of the danger. Even so, many a passman and his bike have ended in the canal, no joke on an early frosty winters morning. Sometimes the resident bridge-man's wife used to open the bridge for us, to allow her husband to rest.

In those days more and more craft were being introduced to the work on the canal, some were brought around the coast from as far afield as Yorkshire. With these craft came men that had to be taught the river outside Sharpness and the canal and river above Gloucester. I mention this because their way of towing was different from ours. We used to use manila hawsers, but they used wire and springs. Where the lock walls were low at Sharpness, it was frightening to see them set a tow wire up. They used to put the eye of the rope spring on the after bollards, run it along the deck of the dumb barge, out through the towing eye, shackle it to the tow wire and on to the motor craft's towing hook. They would then go ahead with the motor and set this wire up, with it whipping and cracking. The quay wall at Sharpness would miraculously clear as men ran to safety in case the wire parted. I had once seen this happen and sever a man's leg. I never, ever found out why they used wires for towing. They were extremely dangerous.

We used to run up the canal in those early years, towing our dumb barges. This could on occasions be hazardous. The man at the helm of the motor craft had to watch the dumb barge behind. Every few minutes he would look out through the rear window of the wheelhouse and the moment the dumb barge took a run, he eased the engine down. This gave the crew of the dumb barge a chance to straighten it out of its run. I will explain what a 'run' is. Perhaps the dumb barge would get too near the port bank. A suction would be caused between the stern of the vessel and the bank, which means the crew had no steerage weigh, and the barge would run across the canal hard into the starboard bank. Anything moored to the bank had no chance. Often I have seen a dumb barge take a run, smash bridges with its plinth and sink moored craft. Other passing craft in the canal

Hosing down prior to scrubbing salt, sand and mud off.

have had dumb craft take a run into them even after they were seen coming and the motor's engine eased to pass in safety. Fenders were used sometimes, but the standard ones were of little help. Consequently we were always making our own fenders. With dumb barges and the cargoes we carried, we really needed fenders for safety reasons, as well as to stop some of the damage.

A typical run up the canal with a loaded pair of tankers, the motor and dumb barge, started at about 4.30 a.m. from the old dock at Sharpness. We used to try to be at Purton bridges for the run up by 5 a.m. As soon as it was light, the first job of the day (except on a frosty or foggy morning) was to scrub the vessel off. This meant putting the deck hose on the motor vessel and scrubbing from bow to stern to get the salt, sand and mud off, which had washed aboard out in the channel. When this was done, each man cooked his own breakfast, then the deck boy cleaned the cabin and washed up. By this time we would have reached Gloucester.

Sometimes, tankermen used to take some stupid risks that have caused injuries or even deaths. Some crew members used to live nearby and would ride bicycles to the nearest bridge to join the craft. The other crew members would get under way from Sharpness, these men would then join them as they were moving through the bridges. They would hoist their bicycles onto their shoulders, have their food and clothes bags in the other hand, then step on board as the vessel came through the bridge. Sometimes they would misjudge and I've seen them drop their bicycles into the canal. I remember one man, actually the skipper, slip and fall between the wall and his craft, he was very lucky to be alive afterwards, because he was rolled between the wall and the barge. He was in agony when the bridgeman pulled him out. When they got him to hospital they found that he had a broken pelvis.

On another occasion, one of the crew went ashore to go shopping. He stepped from the bow of the craft onto the bridge. The engineer was on the stern end holding his bicycle up, but as he took it the engineer slipped, went over the side and was drawn under by the suction of the vessel. He was drowned. These tragedies did not prevent the practice of getting off and

Still scrubbing off.

onto moving vessels. I have to admit that I have often done it myself.

There have been many collisions between craft. One of the worst was on the four mile bend at Elmore, on the canal. An empty vessel was coming down, and a tug was on passage for Gloucester with several craft, one of them was an old wooden barge called the 'Brittania'. This was a sister ship to the 'Spry', an old Severn trow, which is now at the Iron Bridge Museum in Shropshire, undergoing restoration to its former glory. The empty craft was coming down the canal, and the 'Brittania', loaded with wheat, was being towed by the tug 'Stanegarth' to Gloucester. The down craft took a run and she virtually cut the 'Brittania' in two. When they eventually lifted her, she was put in the barge grave yard at Lydney, and has since rotted away. Many old craft were put out onto the banks of the river in several places like Lydney and Purton. Here they were sunk, and then filled with Severn mud and sand to become a protection against the erosion of the banks.

The barge graveyards were a boon to the Severn Catchment Board. It was easy for them to put a vessel up on the bank where it was needed, and knock some planking out to let the tide fill it. The mud would build up around it and make new and wider banking and saved having to build it with rock or granite. In my early tanking life, there were concrete vessels brought in to help move general cargo, and these would be badly damaged in any collision with other craft. As the tankers were in the majority and always on the move, it was invariably one of them that caused a collision. It came to the point when the concrete was beyond repair and so they were also put out in the graveyard. Some of these can be seen at Purton Weir, between the canal and the river Severn.

Later, they started to experiment with piling the banks. At first they used concrete piles but these used to crack, break or crumble, so steel ones were used instead. This proved successful and so they piled the whole length of the canal, making it much easier for us and the passmen. At the same time, the bridges

Winter in the canal.

Traversing the canal after a snow storm.

were being altered to single swing span. This did away with the passmen, and got rid of hold-ups, such as having to wait for a passman to catch up from one bridge to another. The delays were a hazard as it was easy to go aground in a strong wind. It was a terrible job trying to get a vessel off if one went aground. The damage was not only to waterways property, but to the vessels themselves. The propellers hit rock, the filters blocked up with mud and no cooling water could get through to the engines. This caused havoc and sometimes meant a dry dock repair job. The shipyard at Gloucester always had about ten vessels in for repair. Being tankers they had to be steamed out and gas freed, before they could be worked upon.

When larger vessels of two hundred and fifty to four hundred tonnes started to arrive, the smaller ones began to go, and so the canal was not so congested.

During the winter months, the canal was one of the worst places to work. It used to freeze so hard that we had to push our way through the ice. The ropes would freeze as solid as a steel bar. We pushed them down the engine rooms to try to dry or soften them, for with the frost and ice, they were a devil to handle and would snap like a carrot if set up too hard. On board the dumb barges they had to push them down into the bosun's store. There were two towing hawsers, a five inch for canal and river work, and a ten inch diameter for channel work. We could not use gloves, so by the time you had pulled one in, your fingers and hands were extremely cold. Sometimes the ice cut your hands but you did not know it until the circulation came back to your frozen hands.

When the canal had frozen hard, I have walked alongside my vessel while she has been pushing her way through the ice. I remember trying to pass a loaded vessel when I was negotiating the canal and was empty. The ice was piling up in front of him and under the bow of my vessel until it stopped us both. Then we had to get in touch with the nearest bridgeman and have a tug sent to our assistance. He had to break the ice and pull one of us past the other. I can also remember when it was so bad we had to leave Sharpness with large tankers and small ones, including mine, all moored together in one long tow, all with engines running. We also needed two high powered channel

The long tow through ice in the canal.

Standing on the ice in Sharpness Dock between the sterns of the 'Swift' and 'Linnett'.

tugs, the 'Primrose' and 'Resolute', to tow us to Gloucester dock. It took about six hours to pull us and break the ice to get us there. With our engines going, and the tugs pulling, one can imagine the scene. When we reached Gloucester those same two tugs had to turn around and tow another flotilla of craft back to Sharpness that were empty, for sailing to the channel ports.

We used to traverse the canal with light craft and also towing a dumb barge. We very nearly always towed the barge short up. That is, close to the stern of the motor craft. We had a rope from the bow of the dumb barge on to the towing hook, another from the starboard bow of the dumb barge to the port quarter of the motor craft, and then another from port to starboard. This made sure that the barge stopped in its correct place. We then could pass from vessel to vessel by climbing these ropes whilst under way. This had its advantages because we could have the barge men aboard the motor craft and teach them to handle our vessels. No-one needed to steer the dumb barge, except to get them through the bridges.

We used to stay on board some weekends if we could not get home. We had our exercise in the hold of the lighters. Besides other things, I remember us having boxing lessons. One time comes to mind when we were sparring and had a new chap, who had joined us a few days earlier, give us a lesson on boxing. It turned out that he was a Midlands A.B.A. champion! We soon learned when it came to the rough stuff to treat him with a bit of respect.

At Gloucester dock there was a little Mariners Church. On Sunday mornings the rector used to come aboard the craft that we were on and give us a call. He would make a cup of tea, sometimes joining us with a cup himself. He was very good to us all and was affectionately known as Donald Duck. The little church is still there. It is worth a visit by anyone who is interested, as it was built for seamen, rivermen, bargemen and anyone working at the docks.

It was here also, that I first came in touch with canal boatmen. When I first started, there were hundreds of them travelling the canals of the country. Some that I met were very good to know. Of course, whole families used to be aboard these long boats. As the long boats gradually declined, the men of these families

Jammed in the ice waiting for a tug at The Pilot.

would join the lighter barge and tanker firms. Their knowledge of the river was indispensable to us, as they told us tricks of how to work the river above Gloucester, many things we had not heard of or tried. Their knowledge of fresh water work also was phenomenal. I became very friendly with some of these men, then when I became Master of one of the river tankers their help and advice was invaluable to me. Mostly they could neither read or write, but they certainly knew their river and barge work.

It was here at Gloucester dry dock that several vessels were lengthened to carry more cargo. These vessels were cut in half, a prefabricated section put in, and then joined again to increase their carrying capacity. They had the same number of crew men, thereby making them more economical to run.

Chapter Twelve

Gloucester Docks and Onward
Up the Severn

In the days when the lock at Gloucester was hand operated, there were three gatemen. This was because the road bridge over the lock had also to be opened and shut with each locking. One man can now operate the lock or bridge from a control room.

As a young deck boy on fine mornings, I used to sit watching the lock being operated. It never failed to fascinate me as to the number of locks there were in and out. Most of the craft using them were tankers. I have also sat and watched the pigeons fly onto the wall of the warehouse that used to be on the quay wall. This warehouse ran along the west side of the dock from the lock, to the dry dock. The pigeons used to cling to the walls and peck at the cement between the bricks. It was only by asking the old long boatmen that I found out why the birds did this. They told me that cargoes of salt were brought from Droitwich by the old Severn Trows, down the river Salwarp into the Severn, hence into Gloucester dock and unloaded into these warehouses. The salt eventually leaked into the cement between the bricks and this is what had attracted the pigeons.

As our turn came to lock out, we went into the lock and lowered down to the level of the river. Two craft could go into this lock together, so it saved time if this could be done here. As a boy, I had to take my place up on the bow as a look out. From Gloucester lock to the tar works or Sandhurst, the river wound its way with many blind corners from the lock to the Westgate bridge, which was an arch bridge built of stone. It was situated just above the first bad corner from Gloucester quay and not very high or wide. As a look out I had to listen for craft blowing a warning blast coming down the river. If by chance we were near these corners or bridges, we had to wait for the down craft to clear, so that we could navigate up through. Frequently on

The 'Regent Jill' on the stocks for yearly overhaul.

The 'Regent Linnet' approaching Camp Lock, or by its proper name Bevere Lock.

one of these corners, the stern of a craft has been overhanging the deck of a craft coming up river and all the stanchions have been pushed over and bent. In this situation, we had some iron bars and other tackle either to pull them back into some sort of shape, or replace them, as we did carry spares for this sort of occurrence.

The river was very bad from Gloucester lock to Ashleworth. The mud from tides used to settle on the river bottom and we had to push ourselves, and pull the dumb barge up through when the river was low. It was so bad at times, that we had to give the propeller a kick astern, then go ahead again. This reversing action would clear it of sticks, leaves and mud, which choked the propeller up and lost us all power.

If we were lucky enough to lock out and the tide came up the river at the same time as we were negotiating this pound to Tewkesbury, it used to help us no end, by carrying us along. Unfortunately, it worked the other way too. If we had to punch the ebb tide, it took us much longer. I have been on the run on a bore tide and have gone through Tewkesbury lock when the top and bottom gates have all been open, and the water through the lock and over the weir completely level. This happened often, and the long journey to Stourport or Worcester was shortened considerably.

Once we reached Ashleworth, the run then got better. If the weather was fine, it was here that we had to work on deck, chipping, painting, making fenders, or splicing ropes. There was always work to do. It usually took us about two and three quarter hours to Tewkesbury upper lode lock. We wld wend our way up around Wainlodes Hill to Haw Bridge, the Coalhouse, the Salmon draft, where we saw many salmon netted, the Yew Tree Inn, to the boathouse and then on into the Tewkesbury lock.

The lock at Tewkesbury could hold four craft our size. It had a small tidal basin, and so was much larger than the other locks on the river. Again, it was hand operated. The handles on the mechanism for letting the water into and out of the lock were very large and there was one water paddle on each corner of the lock, four in all. There was a ladder let into the gates and as the vessel ran into the lock, one of the crew would step onto this ladder and climb to the top to help operate the lashers, as they were called. We also had to push the gates open by hand. Once the lock was full and the craft started to pull out. The crew members that had gone ashore to help work the lock had to descend the ladder on the other set of gates and come back on board for the next pound – the length between locks.

The steering of these craft was shared by all hands, the skipper steered mainly the bad parts of the river, such as from Gloucester dock to the top of the parting. Then the deck boy under supervision, took over from here to Haw Bridge and then the mate from Haw Bridge to Tewkesbury upper lode lock. This gave a new boy the chance to learn how to steer. They sometimes changed steering lengths with him to teach him where the deep water channel was. How else was he to learn? A good deck boy soon picked it up, and was taught the rule of the river. Sometimes this could not be kept, so the byelaws were disregarded because of the necessity for loaded craft always to be allowed the deeper water. This was a case of an unwritten rule being applied by the river and tanker men to avoid damage. Of course, there were collisions on the river, but this was mainly due to fog or fresh water.

On leaving Tewkesbury upper lode, we carried on for Worcester. Here we passed the mouth of the River Avon at Tewkesbury where Healings Mill had stood for as long as I can remember, and was once fed by grain-carrying craft from Avonmouth. Once we cleared the Mythe bridge, we came to the best part of the river. It is said that the old long boat river men used to fill their water butts out of this part of the river because the bed of the river from the bridge to the corner, for about two or three hundred yards, was full of springs. The water was reputedly pure from this corner up to Queens Hill and the Mythe Water Works was built here for Water extraction.

Here we came to Sandy Point. The river here is an 'S' bend and inside the bights of the bends are sand banks. These we negotiated with great care, then on to Sextons Lode Railway Bridge, now long since demolished. I used to watch the

51

passenger and goods trains travel over this bridge. Just above here a special war ministry depot for aircraft fuel was built underground, known as Ripple depot, which we used to supply from our craft. If we were bound for here, we could run from Gloucester, discharge, and run back again. During the war when I was a deck boy, the army used to practice putting Bailey Bridges across the river below Upton-on-Severn. They were very good to us, if we blew a warning blast on the ship's whistle, a section of the bridge was slipped out enabling us to pass on up. Then they replaced the section in a very short time. Good practice for them I presume.

The river began to get shallow in parts from here on to Worcester. The shallow sections were about eight feet deep in the summer. In later years much larger tanker craft running to Worcester drew about seven feet six inches. We had to ease up through Upton-on-Severn, as there were a lot of river leisure craft moored here. On occasions we moored here ourselves and spent an evening exploring the local hostelries and sampling their beers. Over the years I made many great friends at the different public houses up and down the river, and I still keep in touch with some of them today. We also made many friends with the Yachtsmen, which helped when we had to explain the reason we needed the deep water channel, and could not always follow the byelaws.

As we went up under the new road bridge at Upton-on-Severn, there was another sand bank that we had to navigate with care. So as Master, I took over the helm from the deck boy as was done to me when I was a deck boy. The river wound round here to Hanley Castle, then on to Stoke Hill. Traversing Stoke Hill shallows had to be done with extreme care, for this was a part of the river where the river bed was all rock. This could put a hole in your craft if you went out of the deep water channel and hit it too hard. Next came Severn Stoke and on to the Rhydd, around the Rhydd to Clevelode and on up the five mile hole. A change of helmsman occurred again, the mate having taken over at the five mile hole, approximately five miles from Worcester.

At this point, we came to the first old ford over the river at the Kempsey stretch. On passing through Kempsey Bay, there were the ketch boat moorings with the Severn Motor Yacht Club-house on its starboard bank. There were many vessels moored here, so again we had to cut our speed so as not to break them adrift. Then we came to the mouth of the River Teme, we had to pass sunken long boats here on the starboard bank, put there to stop bank erosion. Now ahead was Worcester Lock. The full run from Tewkesbury had taken us about three hours. There were two locks here at Worcester, but we could only use the larger one of the two. We had to shoot the dumb barge into the lock first. There was a winch to start them out into the top cutting when they were lifted up, or they were pushed out with hook shafts or barge poles, where they had to wait for the motor craft to lock up. Many years later, the other smaller lock was altered to take our smaller tankers, but again this was too late, for we only used it for about four or five years before the tanker traffic began to diminish.

Here the motor barge helped the lock gatemen a little, as we used to put our bow against the centre of the lock gates and push the gate open when the water had reached its level. The reason we used to lock the dumb barge up first was because the cutting at the bottom, or lower level, was very short, because of this we had a job holding the dumb barge up to the lock gates in the usual way. This was also the home of the Severn commission, and vessels used for repair work were kept here in the top cutting, so it was a little congested with craft. Of course, this was before nationalisation and the Commission had been run by a family by the name of Bradley for many years. The dredger was kept here, she was named the 'John Bradley'. This lock was known by us as Worcester Lock, in fact its proper name was Diglis Lock. Another very large oil depot was here, also owned by the Shell Oil Co. We traded here during the days of the Petroleum Board. If the motor craft was bound for Stourport, and the dumb barge for Worcester, he locked up first and carried on, the dumb barge would then lock up and the crew would bow haul her into the oil basin.

From here as Master I had to navigate the pound from Diglis to Bevere, or as it was commonly known, Camp Lock. This was one of the worst pounds to navigate on the whole length of the river. I had to set the rope up gently, take the vessels out into the river, because at the end of the top cutting was some water turbulence. This was due to a large oil basin cut out of the land on the starboard side of the cutting. The water ran down this side of the river and met the water in the head of the cutting, causing the turbulence, which became worse in flood water. Once we were out in the river, we passed the entrance to the Worcester Canal, on up past the Cathedral and then we had to negotiate Worcester Road Bridge.

Now, Worcester Road Bridge has five arches built of stone, the bridge had been twice widened. It was now so wide that as the bow of one of our craft came out of the bridge, the stern was just entering. As our craft were approximaly 100 feet in length, the bridge gave the impression of being a tunnel. Here great care was taken because we had to ease our speed and take the second arch out from the left hand, or port side, as it was the only one with enough water for us.

Moored to the banks from Diglis Lock, upwards on the starboard hand side were lots of small craft. Here between the two bridges there were passenger steamers used for summer pleasure trips up and down the river. The old long boat river men said that the half-mile of river from the race course grandstand up to the Dog and Duck ferry was deeper here than at any other part between Gloucester and Stourport. In some parts of this half-mile there must have been between 25 and 30 feet of water.

As we cleared the Dog and Duck Ferry, we really did start to run into shallow water, this was so bad that we could hear the shingle tinkling beneath us as we progressed northward past the Pitchcroft Water Works.

Here in the upper reaches of the river, navigation became more and more exacting. The dimensions of Bevere Lock were used to determine the size of our craft. The next two locks were slightly larger, so if our craft could negotiate this one, they could manage the next two. In this lock the motor craft would go through leaving the dumb barge tied up, until she was clear. Then the dumb barge would be again hooked up, to the towing barge above the lock, and dragged into the lock by the five inch hawser passing over the top gates. This had the effect of lifting the bow of the dumb barge over the shingle bottom as well as drawing it into the lock. It was such a tight fit that the rudder had to be disengaged and laid flat against the stern. Only then could the lock gates be closed.

We now approach the old lock of the Droitwich canal on the starboard side. Whoever owned and lived at the old lock, transformed the house beyond recognition. The house has been renovated and the lock, though filled with silt is still there, and has been beautifully landscaped.

Just above here is the mouth of the river Salwarp. This takes small yachts, which navigate up to a boat yard alongside the A38 above Worcester. Above the Salwarp we start to run into bad shallow water again, this being the Grimley sand banks on the port side. There are holiday bungalows on the starboard side all built on stilts because of flooding. The scene gives the impression of huts in a Malaysian jungle.

Holt Lock in summer was crowded with spectators watching us work the lock. In later years it was fenced off because of the danger. Holt was always a favourite holiday place for the Midland people.

We left Holt Lock and the deck boy was now put on the wheel for another lesson on towing and steering over shallow water. We cleared Holt top cutting and made our way round the corner to Lenchford Hotel. Here there was a large caravan park, again set on stilts, except for the small ones that could be towed to safety. Next came Shrawley, more shallow water, past Chitters ditch and on to Hampstall, over a very bad shallow rock and on up to Lincombe. We pass another Ministry Depot here, (Lincombe Hall), where little can be seen. Incidentally, I discharged the very first cargo into this place. The Lincombe Lock was our last lock, and it had a great significance as to the amount of cargo we carried to Stourport-on-Severn depots. We had to wriggle our way into this lock here by running the engines at half speed, then turn the wheel from port to starboard and back again, repeating this until we were in the lock. To get out of the lock after lifting up, we had to move very slowly because we were actually touching the lock sill. Every morning, the lock keeper used to take the water reading off the top sill water level board. This was sent through to Gloucester to the petroleum board or the carriers, and in turn relayed to the

'Regent Jill' entering Lincombe lock loaded, taken from the centre of the top gates.

'Regent Lark' discharging on the oil berth at Stourport-on-Severn.

skippers loading at Avonmouth. If there was say, six feet two inches of water, we could get over the sill with a draft of six feet. Provided we moved out steadily and slowly, and did not suck down on to the sill, which could happen if we tried to go fast. This damaged both the sill and the vessel's bottom.

After the same procedure of locking up, we moved on up past the timber yards and general cargo jetties to the depot for discharging. The cargo was checked with whatever was on our ullage or cargo sheets. We then connected to the shore lines. This was an operation within itself, with the river running down and us trying to lift a large pipe for connection flange to flange, it was a devil of a job. I once saw a man lose a finger between these flanges as they came together. We had to get somewhere near opposite, then turn the wheel to bring the vessel either in or out to meet it, so as to bolt them together. This was a very tricky job, and had to be done with great care.

When we arrived at Stourport in those days, it was nothing to find several craft waiting to discharge. We had to wait our turn, which could be at any time during the day or night. Someone had to stand by the craft until it was empty then he returned to his bunk until sailing time, which again could be from 5.30 a.m. onwards.

To get away from the depot, you had to swing round and face down river. The width of the river was barely a length and a half of our craft, so we had to swing on the jetty posts by putting a rope around it and back around the stern of our vessel. Then we could let the bow lines go and swing out on the rope. When the motor was half way round, she could slip the line and keep the prop turning ahead to let her continue on round. The dumb barge would have started swinging just before. It would be three quarters of the way round when the motor would drop alongside, pick up the tow rope, fast forward and away we would go to Lincombe Lock for our journey back to Gloucester and then Avonmouth. Lock to lock down river did not give us so much concern, as being light ships, we did not draw too much water and when the river was low, the journey was usually uneventful. The river was at its lowest during the summer months.

Several of these trips had their amusing moments. One day a

long boat making for Lincombe Lock passed us just outside the cutting. I was then just a boy, but I was certain that we had the right of way to lock up first. I had never come up against a husband and wife team on a long boat before. As we passed them, I heard for my first time a woman utter bad language. I could not even now repeat her graphic account of what she wanted to do to my skipper with the boat hook she had on board. She did not like us passing them so close to the lock and had clearly told us so, because they then had to wait for two locks to be made before they could lock up.

Another occasion was when we were approaching a lock. As we had priority over pleasure craft, one that also wanted to lock up was ordered to stay back until we had cleared the lock. He did so, but he was close to the bottom of the Island and as we passed, we drew the water away. This made his vessel sit on the bottom close in shore. He told his wife to push them back with a hook shaft. She did this, but was unfortunate enough to lose hold and leave it standing in the river bed. He was angry at his wife for leaving the hook shaft where it was. Whether in his rage, he thought he had his trunks on under his shorts we did not know. He pulled off his shorts, held his nose and jumped stark naked over the side, into only two feet of water. Every on-looker including ourselves on the tanker saw the funny side of the incident and gave him a resounding cheer.

One frightening thing happened as we were approaching Worcester Bridge, empty and bound for Gloucester. The motor craft bow was always high out of the water and we could never see over it properly. We had to look out of the wheelhouse at one side or the other, but with a bridge in front you could see and aim for the centre of the arch because this was above and ahead of you. We did this as usual, but that day we happened to have a crew man painting up for'ard. When we entered the bridge hole, we were shocked to see him pull a girl up over one side of the bulwarks and a boy over the other. There had been a rowing skiff in the bridge hole and we had cut it in half. The couple in the boat had jumped and made a grab for our bulwark. The crewman had caught hold of the girl's hands and dragged her and then the boy on board. They were very lucky to be alive.

Another thing I could never understand was why many fishermen would get as near to the waters edge as possible to fish. Some we could see, but others used to hide behind the bushes or willow trees. In the latter years the solo motor pulled the water out into the river harder and farther, which returned with a very heavy rush. So if we did not see the anglers, we did not ease our speed and the water would go up to around their waists as they sat there on their fishing tackle baskets. If we saw them, we eased our engines. If they saw us approaching people with rowing boats or skiffs without realising the danger, used to row up under the overhang of trees. As we went by we would shout at them to tell them to keep rowing rather than to pull under the bushes, because although we had eased down the engines, we still drew the water. As it went back, it would push the small boats up into the branches. Very alarming for the occupants of these small boats. Why the hire people did not warn them about this hazard we will never know.

We used to moor at many places on the river. Usually we preferred to tie-up outside a pub. One was the Wharf Hotel at Holt. One summer evening I made an arrangement for the Landlord to keep the landing stage clear for me to moor, as we were going to spend the night there, when we arrived back empty going down river. As the water flow was down, I had to swing around and head into the stream to moor with just my bow on the jetty.

Here after the pub was closed, the landlord, his large family and my crew would often go swimming. I used to rig lights up around the bow, put a ladder overside and away we would go. On this occasion, there was a hired yacht moored ahead of me, of which there were many on the river. The master had watched me swing my vessel in the confines of the river and moor up. He congratulated me on the way I did this, and asked if my crew and I would have supper with him and his wife and family, two boys and a girl about of 18-22 years of age. We had a very enjoyable meal followed by a swim in the river. We sat talking afterwards and this gentleman said to me, 'We have had an evening to remember, and when I saw you swing your vessel around in the river. I thought I haven't a man on board my ship that could do that.' When I asked him what ship he was speaking

Entering Tewkesbury lock bound to Stourport-on-Severn.

of, he replied, 'I'm the Captain of the 'Illustrious'.

In the top reaches of the Severn there were very short lengths between Worcester, Bevere, Holt and Lincome Locks, and very often if you caught up with slow moving craft you blew to pass. Sometimes passing was impossible unless you came to a part of the river that was both wide enough and deep enough to do so. If it was a tug with one barge in tow and the skipper was in a hurry, he would feign that he had not heard you, for if he could keep you behind him he would. Then he would not have to wait at the next lock to lock up. However, you would have to wait for two locks. This did not deter us because we had a trick we could play. We would get our vessel up close to his dumb barge's stern end, drop our bow against it just on its quarter, go ahead and push against it. The crew of the dumb barge then could not steer. It would then veer away, go into the trees or the bank and the tow rope would part. We would then go astern, round the after end of the dumb barge and away. Many is the timber lighter that has lost part of its cargo over side. The river dwellers and lock keepers, must at these times have had a good store of timber out of the river. Sometimes it came to fisticuffs between the tug skipper and the lighter crews for not easing their engines and observing the river byelaw that faster craft should pass by. I often wondered what was written into their damage reports. The tug skipper and the barge skipper would have had to write one each.

Chapter Thirteen

Rough Weather

As our tankers were flat bottomed we always had to be wary of rough weather. Every wave we hit or landed on shuddered and shook us very badly. I have been out only once in a force ten gusting to eleven. This was storm to hurricane force. I shall never forget the occasion.

The vessel I was on was the 'Regent Jill', a solo craft. We had engine trouble on the return journey to Sharpness from Avonmouth, due to the rough weather on the tide before. As we left Sharpness I was told that the wind was force eight. However, the forecast was for it to increase later but this half of the message didn't reach the 'Regent Swallow', the 'Wandale H' and myself. We were the only three vessels to sail that night.

We sailed about eleven thirty and the tide was running with the wind. At that time the sea was not too bad, but when the tide turned and the wind was against the tide, things began to worsen. I pumped ballast into my fore and aft peak, and also into the cofferdams which gave some stability. The further down channel towards Avonmouth we went the worse the weather became. When we cleared Beachley, we were in the lee of the Welsh shore, but when we opened up the channel across to Avonmouth from Charston we certainly hit the heavy seas. We could not turn round and had to carry on for Avonmouth. We crossed Kingroad crab fashion from the Welsh to the English shore. The coastguard at Avonmouth was watching us, and so were the Harbour Master and lockgate men. As I approached the entrance of Avonmouth lock, they opened the gates, let me in, closed them behind me then took my mooring ropes afterwards. With the gates closed, we were sheltered and were not dancing up and down in the heavy sea. They did the same with the 'Regent Swallow' and 'Wardale H'. When they had lifted the lock up, and we were level with the lock wall, a deputation of Harbour Master and Haven Master were waiting for us. They wanted to know why we had sailed in such bad weather. The Master of the 'Wardale H', had to make a written report because they had seen him being blown around and had appeared to be in great difficulties. Myself and the Master of the 'Regent Swallow' had not had too much trouble but believe me, it was very hard work handling those craft in that weather on that night. When we checked after mooring in the oil dock, the cabin was a shambles; bottles of sauce and other things were smashed and scattered. We had lost our spare anchor overside, the lifeboat had moved against the wheelhouse and several other small things that had been lashed on deck were missing. That was one night the crews of those three vessels will never forget.

The experiences in rough weather were many, but in war time we had to sail whether we liked it or not. Because we were towing, we spent many an hour somewhere ashore between Sharpness and Avonmouth as we could not make it out into the strong side winds. If when we got to Shepperdine the wind was extra strong, and we knew we could not make it, we would deliberately put ashore on the mud flats. When the tide had receded we would put on sea boots and squelch up the mud to the high shore with shoes tied round our necks. There we would change into our shoes leaving our sea boots, lying down to keep dry inside if it rained walk down the shore to the local pub called the Windbound, which seemed to be open all hours in those days. The landlord of the pub always made us river men welcome. We could always be sure of a meal or a ploughman's lunch with our beer.

When I was Master of the 'Regent Swift', a solo craft unable to tow, and with a low powered engine of only 95 h.p.; I decided to sail one day from Sharpness to Avonmouth. The wind up channel was gale force eight, gusting to nine, which I learned later had increased to storm ten. We pumped in two cargo tanks of water to give us ballast, for the weather was always worse from Beachley or the Lyde to Avonmouth. The wind was south-westerly blowing up channel and the tide was ebbing. The wind was therefore, against the tide, which always made conditions worse. We tried three times to get around the Lyde, the moment we cleared the Chapel Island, the wind blew us round and off course. As much as I tried to keep her head to wind the more we were blown back. The last time I had tried, I found I had to give up, so this time I decided to turn round and run for cover under Slimeroad cliff. I eased the engine (she was deck controlled) and gave the mate instructions to put all the speed on when I gave the word. I watched her rise and fall with the sea and when I saw my chance I told the mate to wind her up to full speed. She wallowed, rose and then swung. On the binnacle table was a very thick and heavy glass ash tray, which shot across the wheelhouse, into a steel bulkhead and smashed into tiny pieces. We eventually got round and ran for cover, then went ashore at Slimeroads, under the lee of the cliff and in front of the leading lights.

I remember years before, the men who had taught me about the river had told me there was an imaginary line across as regards the tides. This was from Oldbury Pill to Slimeroad. On the low tides, the water ran out of the river above the line faster than a big tide, and below slower. They also told me that it was opposite on a big tide, i.e., the water ran out slower above the line and faster below it. The shape of the river at Aust and Beachley, acts as a bottle neck. This is why in very bad weather on large tides it makes very bad seas at that point. Bearing in mind we were only on small craft, we really had some rough times out there. I have known deep-sea men to be very frightened aboard these small craft. Some have given up and gone back to deep sea work. They used to say it was safer, the movement of large craft being very different from that of small vessels in heavy sea.

After clearing the Lyde into Slimeroads.

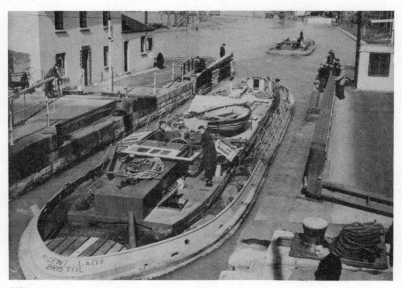

History was made when these tankers went through Gloucester Lock. From docks to river without stopping, 2nd April 1955.
By courtesy of Gloucester Citizen.

Chapter Fourteen

Fog

Many is the day or night we have left Avonmouth for Sharpness with the weather getting worse as we went up the channel. Of course we were not able to predict this and that is where the times and courses we used to take, stood us in good stead. November's fogs were the worst, we all dreaded this sort of weather.

As a boy, I was taught to look out for different marks in the river as we approached them. If we had passed them according to our running time, the skipper would confirm this and then give us the next mark to look for. I have stood for hours up forward as look out. In freezing weather I have been so cold I have had a hard job to get warm again. Our feet seemed always to become the coldest. I have been dressed in layers of overcoats, balaclavas, scarves and gloves and still become miserably cold. Fog would freeze white on our clothes, as on trees in winter. We used to fold the front of the wheelhouse down so that the helmsman could have a better view and it enabled us to talk to one another as well.

When anyone tells you that your scalp could crawl with fright, believe me that is quite correct. When I first experienced foggy weather, I was a boy on board the 'Regent Jill'. We were towing the 'Regent Jack', and when we left Avonmouth for Sharpness we always ran with the tide. As we left Avonmouth, the visibility was bad. I was on the forward deck as look out when the fog began to get thicker. I remember the chief coming forward and saying conditions were going to get worse and to keep a sharp look out. The skipper told me to look out for the first perch in Kingroad. Well, we missed that in the fog and I was told to look out for the second one. This I did, eventually he informed me that we had run long enough, so we had missed that one also, and next to keep a look out for Charston Rock, which had a lighthouse upon it. The chief came forward with me, and I

The 'Regent Robin' about to enter the Haw Bridge in flood water, taken from the deck of 'Regent Swift'.

The 'Regent Jill' running into Worcester Bridge hole. A most dangerous manoeuver in flood water. No room for errors.

could hear running water, and saw a run of tide, but it was too late. The fog had become so thick by this time. The skipper was too far to the westward of his course and we had run below, or bottom side, of Charston Rock. The tide pushed us against the rock, we were swung by the tow rope around it and came to rest facing up river, and the dumb barge facing down river. The next thing I knew, the mate shouted to the dumb barge crew to take in the tow rope as he was going to slip the towing hook. He told the crew, to keep shouting and we would pick them up the other side, where the tide would take them. As this was the first time I had been in a situation like this, I was amazed at the risks taken. However, we did slip the rope, and indeed picked them up again, to continue up the river to Sharpness. Being so young and green to this part of the job, I didn't worry so much as I did when I got older. I then realised how bad and dangerous the river could be.

By this time I had begun to study the river, learned how and what to look for to understand the runs of the tide. This consisted of observing debris being taken by the tide with speed, or watching the way water ran off rocks or sandbanks. If there was no debris, to be able to tell a tide run by looking for something specific, then in fog conditions, we would have a good idea where the tide run had come from. As the years went by, there were more obstacles in the river as the Berkeley Power Station, Oldbury Power Station, cooling lake and the Severn Bridge were built. These also caused us concern and even tide runs came off these. So if you were near them, and you had an idea of your position, you could know that you had passed them, for the flow of the water was broken by these obstacles. There were other things as well, such as a blind perch half way across the river between Inward Rocks on the western side of the river, and the Shepperdine on the east. This in later years was replaced by a buoy with a bell fixed to it. At Shepperdine, the light keeper's garden was the site of the first bell in this vicinity, and by blowing four blasts on the ship's siren, he could put it on for the vessels out in fog. Also, if things were extremely bad, you could use the sound of this bell to go ashore on the mud flats where the vessels could lie in safety until the next tide, or until the fog lifted.

'Regent Lady' dropping down through Worcester Bridge.
By courtesy Worcester Evening Post.

'Regent Swift' pushing up through Worcester Bridge.

Incidentally, this fog bell at Shepperdine had a history of its own. We used to blow for it to be rung in fog, either to go ashore or to give us an idea of where we were. It had been the bell of a full rigged ship called Atlas, built near Hull in 1812 and broken up in 1832. The bell then spent some years on Gloucester dockside to start the dockers to work. Then it was fitted to the back light at Shepperdine in about 1941. It has been taken back to Gloucester dock and is to be re-hung in the dock area.

When the cofferdam for Berkeley Power Station was built, a siren was installed upon it to give us a warning. Also, at Lydney they had a gong on the pier and there was a large bell on Sharpness pier.

The worst and most tragic accident I well remember, was on the night of October the 5th, 1960, when the Severn Railway Bridge was demolished by two tankers. There were many tankers and general cargo craft bound for Sharpness, just how many I don't know, but there were four locks up from the basin to the dock before they were cleared.

The Weather when we left Avonmouth was clear and it was a very high tide so everyone was trying for first lock. As we approached Berkeley Power Station there didn't seem to be any lights up towards Sharpness and I began to get apprehensive. Suddenly, we ran into dense fog. I could barely see the bow, there were several craft ahead of me and they all began to give warning blasts on their sirens. I did the same. I knew our position to be above Berkeley Pill so I turned my vessel into the soft mud somewhere by Sanigar Pill and there I lay, holding against the mud and facing southward. I decided to wait until some of the other craft had docked, which would give me the chance to get my vessel into Sharpness without the risk of colliding with any of them.

With the siren on the pier, the sirens aboard the craft and the engines hammering against a lage tide, it was very noisy. Now, as to what happened next, this is my theory.

The 'M.V. Arkendale H' carrying black oil and the 'M.V. Wastdale H' carrying petrol, either overran or were taken up past Sharpness North Pier by the tide. They were somewhere up near the old dock, continually blowing their sirens at intervals and were steadily drifting farther up the river. We all knew once you had got up past the pier, the pier siren could not be heard because it was boxed in and had a grill on its south side, to direct the sound southwards.

Whether the masters of these two vessels thought its siren had been switched off and edged toward one another to shout and ask each other what to do, or where they thought they were, I don't know. If they had, they may have moved too close and their vessels sucked together by the water turbulence. I have seen this happen often. The flat bottomed and straight sided tankers set up a powerful suction. The drifting tankers must have been close up to the bridge. Most of the other skippers and I, by this time, had docked and was up on the quay wall, when we all heard a terrific explosion. As my craft was safely moored I made my way to the old Sharpness Dock. When I got there I could see two spans of the bridge down and a raging fire. The heat of the fire from the oil and a fractured gas main that was laid across the bridge had cleared the fog and gave a clear view of the terrible scene. I could hear men crying for help but there was nothing we could do. We felt so helpless.

One skipper, whose vessel was in the basin, managed with volunteers to commandeer a light rowing boat. He loaded it onto a small lorry, took it to Purton, and with the help of another man rowed out into the river and found and saved one of the crew. The two skippers swam ashore to safety on the Lydney side. Seven other men lost their lives.

There were different parts of the river that were safe havens and had soft bottoms to lie on. Often in fog, we had to find these places and go ashore until the next tide. At night it was safer to stop or find a safe anchorage. Some of these places were Mathern Ouze at the mouth of the Wye, and Slimeroads, Shepperdine, but there were places that craft had to run aground and had to stay until next tide. If you did run aground on an ebbing tide, within fifteen minutes there was no water around the vessel.

Early morning spring fogs rolling off the fields to drift across the river were a terror too. These fogs could come as daylight came, or appear in the evening as the light was fading. Once I remember it rolling in off the shore with an early morning frost when we had left Sharpness bound for Avonmouth. I had heard

'Regent Wren' pushing up through Worcester Bridge. Note the power station which has since been demolished.

Regent Robin pushing up through Worcester Bridge.

that if you could get high enough it was possible to see above it. So I shinned up the mast and sat on the mast head light. Sure enough, I could see far. It was like looking down at clouds from an aeroplane window. I had been up there for about half an hour and we were somewhere in the region of Fishing House lights just below the Power Station at Berkeley, when I saw another mast cutting through the mist. It was heading towards our starboard side and was about a quarter of a mile away. We had earlier heard another vessel blowing and it must have been this one which was bound up river and loaded. I shouted to our crew to turn to port. On the other craft they also had lookouts on board and must have heard me, so they turned to port as well to run with the tide. We turned towards the shore and passed within about forty feet of each other, but luckily we didn't collide. It wasn't very often that we were as fortunate. Of course, running on times and courses as we did, we had to try to rectify the difference to regain our station.

As time passed more solo vessels appeared on the river and life became easier, because we did not have to worry about the men on the end of the tow rope. But more craft on the river meant more chances of collisions, and being oil carrying gave us more cause to worry. Once I was involved in a very bad collision in Slimeroads. This was in fog, at night, and with a big tide. I remember this night very clearly, not only for the collision but also because of the events leading up to it. We went down to the lock at Avonmouth, and sailing that tide for Sharpness was the tug 'Resolute', with one cargo barge in tow, and another tanker, the Darleydale. Nothing else would sail, because of the bad weather. Well, we had made up our minds to sail, deciding that visibility was good enough to be able to pick up some of the river marks. I pulled out of the dock first and set my initial course across Kingroad to Charston Rock Light, and keeping a sharp look out I picked it up. Then I set course for the Chapel Rock, and found this also. Then the weather seemed to worsen. I rounded the Lyde and went into Slimeroads. Here I decided that we were much too early to run on. I could just make out the Slimeroad Navigation lights. I swung my vessel round head to tide, got them in line and stayed there waiting for the tide to make and give me more water to Sharpness, with less chance of

The Old Westgate Road Bridge at Gloucester.

Haw Bridge before the tragedy.

The dredger helping to clear up the debris from the demolished bridge.

Tewkesbury Abbey taken from the deck of a tanker across the flooded meadows.

hitting a sand bank. My lookout and I saw the 'Darleydale' come in and swing round just astern of my vessel. The tug 'Resolute' and tow followed in, and did the same between my vessel and the navigation lights. Here we all held, and it was approximately three hours to flow at Sharpness. I waited an hour steaming into the tide and at two hours to flow and decided to make a run for it. The fog had lifted a little, making visibility much better, so I turned my vessel to port to open the navigation lights and give me room to swing around. When I had them wide open, and bearing in mind the large strong tide, I started to swing. Well, the Master of the 'Darleydale' did the same, when he realised I was going to make a run for it. In doing so he had forgotten the strength of the tide and he should have waited for me to clear the area. By not doing so he steamed into my port side ripping into my after No. 3 tank. I can see the sparks now as her bow cut into my vessel. With the impact, the water came aboard. As we only had free board of about nine inches, my cargo of four-star petrol began to flow out of the tank. I now had to be more than careful because of the danger of explosion. I had to hang off Sharpness until nearly high water, then notify the Harbour Master by hailing the pier that I was badly damaged. We did not have wireless or ship to shore. He locked up the tug, his tow and also the 'Darleydale'. I then had to make my way slowly into the basin and moor alongside the jetty. While this was going on, there were many lookouts and watchmen placed to stop anyone lighting a match or doing anything else silly. If anything had happened to ignite the fumes, half of Sharpness would have gone up in flames. Besides, I still had three tanks full of petrol, somewhere in the region of 100 tons.

Running down the river to Avonmouth I've often turned up to tide with other Masters to sail for Avonmouth. Many is the time that ten, twelve or even fifteen Masters have gathered at the head of the south pier at tide time to see if it was worth taking the chance of sailing for Avonmouth. The discussion was the visibility, the chances of it clearing, or if we could see to pick marks up the river. When running down the river to Avon-mouth in the early days when towing, and if the tide was high enough, we could go 'south about', as it was termed, i.e., follow the shore line down. This was a dangerous thing to do. On one occasion I was on lookout with a couple more crew members when we heard someone shouting 'Turn her off'. I immediately shouted 'Hard to starboard' to the skipper. This he did and I looked back round to see a man with a wheelbarrow standing on the sea wall at Fishing House. It was he who shouted at us and saved us from running into the wall. It turned out that he was a River Board man repairing the brick work. Another time, I was told, another vessel was running down inshore and got too close to Oldbury Lake, he found out because he had run through the salmon putchers, which were popping up all round the vessel.

When the ferries were running across the river between Aust and Beachley, another craft was running down this way and had picked up Aust cliff. He set his vessel off to pick up Northwich bouy. The skipper, after running a little time, shouted to his lookout, 'Can you see anything?' 'Yes' he said, 'there is a man running alongside us and he's calling you names!' The man was scrubbing the mud off the ferry landing pier. He had heard them coming through the fog and had started running up the pier for the shore. It seems that the ebbing tide had brought the vessel down close as it was running out for the buoy, and it had missed the pier by two yards.

We made many friends among the yacht owners, who mostly belonged to the Severn Motor Yacht Club. One of them came drinking with us one evening at Sharpness. He was not going down channel on this particular holiday, as it was late in the year. Instead, he asked one of the tanker skippers if he would take him to Avonmouth and back again the next day, for that was where we were bound. I was sailing that morning and tide time was around eight o'clock, which was ideal for him. Next morning he duly arrived, but so did dense fog. We discussed whether to sail or not. Some sailed and some did not. I was one that did. I warned the other skipper about his passenger, but he said he was going to take the yachtsman and said that he believed, he would be O.K. So, I sailed, maintained my times and courses and duly arrived at Avonmouth. We then had to wait until the other vessels arrived. The Harbour Master was just making preparations to finish tide as everyone was in the lock except, yes, you've guessed it, the one with the passenger on board. Then we heard a blast on a ship's whistle and he arrived into the entrance and on into the lock. He had been in trouble. It was high tide and he decided to come down shore, but had misjudged his last run and had nearly hit Hills Flats buoy. This had made the passenger very nervous. They ran on down without seeing anything else, until they were nearly at Avonmouth. North of Avonmouth pier was an old iron pier, used for discharging sea going tankers during the war and now disused. If you can visualise the square formed by the upright pillars, with the water as the base and the pier deck as the top, within alternate squares an 'X' shaped iron girder for strengthening. It seems that he had somehow got behind this pier and had no other alternative but to try to get through a square without the 'X' girders. He managed this but caught his port side, holing his vessel on an upright and his mast was carried away. The yachtsman was shaken so much that when they docked at Avonmouth he got on shore and said to the skipper 'No way am I coming back with you. Where do I catch the bus?'

Many months after, I met him socially at Upton-on-Severn and we were swapping river yarns. Well, the story he told of what happened that foggy day I will never forget. We very often heard him tell other yacht owners that it was much safer to spend their time north side of Sharpness lock. He also declared that in all his days, he was then in his fifties, he had never been so terrified as he was on that trip, but that he would always hold us tanker men as the best, bar none, on the river.

Accidents were very few, somewhere in the region of two per cent, for we ran that river so much that we had our own way of navigating in fog. All I do have to say is that those men that work the river now in bad or foggy weather, don't know they are born. They have radar, sound equipment, radio and all the mechanical aids to navigate that river. All we had was a compass, a clock and a hell of a lot of river knowledge, but most of all a lot of luck. I often sit and wonder how the old trow men got about the river in fog, or didn't they? I don't think we will ever know. As for us in the tankers, well we did get about the river outside Sharpness, and how!

In the last few years there was a coastal tanker that used to come to Gloucester occasionally for repairs, and she was fitted with radar. The Master was a local man and having been through the mill, knew what we had to do in fog. He used to have us alongside in this sort of weather and take us to Avonmouth. How uncanny it was too, for by looking at the screen we knew just where we were and what was happening, and if he was bound for Swansea he would heave to, off Avonmouth to give us a compass fix off the radar screen and we would go right in between the piers when he released us.

Chapter Fifteen

Fresh or Flood Water Above Gloucester

When I first started on the river, the Westgate Road Bridge over the Severn at Gloucester was a stone arch. When the flood water was about 16ft or 17ft at Gloucester Lock we would have difficulty getting through. Later, the bridge was demolished and replaced by a steel one, with so much head room it was no longer any trouble to us.

There were two ways of getting through these bridges; we could, 'run them'. Which meant going through the bridge down river at speed. This could be very dangerous. Or we could drop down through stern first, using the engine and ropes on bollards on shore. In those days we used to tow, so we had to liaise with the dumb barge skipper to se what he wanted to do. Of course, if we ran the bridge we were through in a couple of minutes. It was just hard luck if we hit anything, and there were times when we did. The second way took time. We had to prise things such as pipe lines, or the rope leads, or bollards to avoid getting them getting caught, until eventually we dropped clear of the bridge. I have seen hatchways and bicycles hung over the side of craft where they have been on deck and would have caught against the bridge.

Years ago at the old Westgate bridge there was a man who used to earn his living by dropping craft down through stern first. He had a full coil of 3½" rope and a wheelbarrow. We would enter the parting at the tar works or Sandhurst. Here there was a board telling us the height of water at Gloucester lock. Knowing how high our vessel stood, we could work out what was the best thing to do. If we had to drop, we had to swing round.

About half a mile above the railway bridge was a bay in the port bank. We got the dumb barge alongside before this, ran our bows into this bay so the two craft swung around to face up the river, then dropped gently with the flow of the water to the

80

bridge holes. Here the man on shore was ready with his rope. He used to pass the eye of the rope to us and we put it on our bow bollards and out through the bow lead. He would then take a turn round the mooring bollard on shore and gently drop us through the bridge. Once we were through Westgate bridge, we had to drop down onto Gloucester quay and on into the dock before we were able to swing round again.

If we decided to run the bridge, we had to be sure of a clear run down through the bridges, and had to know what clearances we had. Here, I had another lesson from an old longboatman, that could only be done on board a dumb barge when empty. The trick was to get everything flat down. The wheelhouse was let down flat on the deck and the cabin hatch and bicycles if they were on board hung over the side. The only thing left standing up on deck was the steering wheel and gypsy, the part carrying the pulleys and chains. The old river man showed me how a couple of times until I had learnt it. He used to take the nut and washer off the steering wheel, then take the two nuts off the bolts at the bottom of the gypsy and draw the bottom bolt right out. Then just before we reached the bridge he would steer the craft and line her up for the centre of the hole of the bridge. The mate would then, as she entered the bridge, pull the bottom bolt out, the skipper would push the steering wheel off, and then quickly lie flat on the deck, along with the mate and the deck hand. The bridge would then be about one foot six inches above us as she went through.

When we were through, the gypsy would be picked up, the bolts slipped in, the steering wheel put on, the key pushed in, then we were back to normal in a couple of minutes. I have done this myself many times.

When we left Gloucester we had to punch this flood water up to Stourport-on-Severn. To get up the river we had to use the slack water or we could not make much headway. When running in the river the fastest flow is always on the outside of the bight or bend. For example, if the bend went round to the right, the fastest flow of the water was on the left or port side of the river. So you kept your vessel up behind the corner where the water did not run so fast. In doing so you had to weave from one side of the river to the other to get behind these corners to keep in the slack water.

Once, when the river was full of water, the Severn Traveller was towing a dumb barge to Worcester. It had got to Sandy Point, where the river was at its fullest with flood water. You could see Sexton's Lode Railway Bridge but no river bank, only bushes. This man had been steering up towards this area and could see the bridge ahead. At this point there were two bushes about a width of the river apart and he steered between them for the bridge. What he didn't know, as he was new to the job, was that the river had an 'S' bend at this point, and he had to steer round this before he got to the bridge. Well, the outcome was, his bow was against the bank. He didn't go anywhere for half an hour until the skipper came up on deck from his midday meal. He realised what had happened and had to get his craft back on to her proper course. Apart from losing half an hour's steaming time, nothing else was lost and no damage done.

Going on from Gloucester to Tewkesbury we had to make a choice of either going over the weir or through the lock. We had special marks for this, and would ask at Gloucester lock what the water heights were at all the locks, for example we would ask 'What is the water at Tewkesbury?' The answer could be 'Seven foot on the top sill and rising an inch an hour'. It would take us approximately three and a half to four hours to get to Tewkesbury and we then knew there was 7ft 4" on the weir, which gave enough water to punch up over it to save time by not locking up.

Coming down the other way empty or with ballast, one could always tell what water was on the weir by the Mythe Bridge. If the water was up to the joint of the combing stone (the bridge iron work was built on this) we had water over the weir. Anything less and you had to make sure what you were drawing. To give yourself more clearance to go safely over the weir, you could let the ballast out of the after peak and ballast tank, which would lift her stern up about six inches. When we were going over the weir, especially if the water on the weir was only just deep enough, we had to ease engines back so that she did not pull herself down onto the weir. We would drift over, then start the pumps to put ballast back in again. We would do this day and night, which is where the headlights came in handy, for at night we could shine onto the combing stones at the bridge to see the water level. Anything lower than that and we had to use the lock.

I remember running back like this one night and the lock keeper at Tewkesbury upper lode was waving a red light to us to ease down. This we did and the mate went forward to hear what the keeper had to say. He warned that a vessel called the 'Darleydale' had knocked the Haw Bridge down. I did not believe him, one arch maybe, but not all three arches of the Old Haw Bridge. I decided to carry on down. The keeper must have been in touch with the police, for when I got to the Coal House or what is known as the White Lion above the bridge, I could see lights flashing at me over the fields. I decided to swing round and stop. I was doing about eight knots and the water speed was the same. So in total I suppose I was heading down river at about sixteen knots.

I eased my speed, turned her into the port bank, headed into the tide and held her. I dropped across the river to the port bank by the farm house as I was now facing up river. In the headlights on my bow I saw a large tree and we moored up to it. When we were moored I walked forward and met a Police Sergeant and Constable on shore who informed me that the 'Darleydale' had indeed collided with the bridge. It had collapsed on to her wheelhouse, killing the Master. It had twisted the pillar and all three bridge arches had collapsed.

I was thankful I had not carried on down the river as I would have surely been involved in the pile up.

It seemed to me that the skipper of the 'Darleydale' had somehow taken the wrong arch and gone at the bridge too slowly. The water had pushed the vessel down under the starboard side of the cast iron arch. It had fractured and the whole lot had collapsed upon him. He had I believe taken it too slowly, for when running bridges, speed was essential. After that episode I am still alive to tell this tale, and I am thankful to those policemen for that.

We carried on from Tewkesbury to Worcester. At Worcester, or Diglis weir, we had our marks to follow for the weir below the lock. This was a set of drains, one above the other, built into the bank with brick work and we could take marks from these. Once over the weir we then had to negotiate the worst obstacle of all, this was the Worcester Road Bridge. As we approached the Diglis Hotel we kept an eye on the quay wall on the river bank. If the water was up to the top stone, (which, I may add was coloured black and all the rest were red), we knew that we could go over the weir.

We have run Worcester Bridge the same as the old Westgate Bridge, by kicking the wheel off, but only without water ballast. As the years went by and the dumb barges were taken off the river above Gloucester, it was only motor craft that went to Stourport. I knew that when the water was 21ft 6" at Worcester lock, even the tankers could not get through because as the water rose, the arch got smaller in height and width.

I remember once coming down into Bevere lock. It was always understood that the hand rail on the bottom gates was a very good mark for the height of the bridge hole. If your vessel stood just below or level with this rail, she would go through. Well, I came down this trip with the 'Regent Jill' loaded with water and I could not get any more on board. The river water was across our deck amidships and we were as low as we could possibly get her. I stepped on to the lock wall and asked the lock keeper what the water was at Diglis Lock. He said the height was 22ft 6" . According to what I had learnt, this was past the limit for negotiating it. This is where the old river men knew more than I did, and I had another lesson from them here.

The two lock keepers were ex-longboat men, bred and brought up on the river. They told me that the 'Regent Swift' and 'Severn Rover' above the bridge on the quay, could not get through, but that if I had the nerve, they said, I could. Laughingly I asked how they thought I could while the others couldn't. They explained what I had to do. It sounded feasible enough, so as it was daylight, decided to have a go.

The highest part of my vessel that day was my steering wheel. Everything else was flat to deck level and I had left my lifeboat at Gloucester dock on the way up, so we were totally uncluttered. Of course, I was on the way down for another trip which meant extra money to myself, my crew and of course, the firm. I cast off and started down river. My mate had a camera on board and said he would take a photograph, so I told him to keep clear of me and not to forget to duck as I ran for the bridge hole. When I got down to the Dog and Duck ferry, half way up the racecourse length, I started to do as I had been told by the lock keepers. I had to take all speed off her and let her go quietly, losing speed as far as the railway bridge. When I got through the railway bridge I had to pile all the power and speed on to her. As the old river men said, she would still be making speed as she entered the bridge. I could not believe what happened next. As she entered, the bow started to go down, the after end lifted up, I could see through the balustrade, then the after end started to go down. By this time I was on my knees in front of the steering wheel. My mate took his photograph, then dived on to the deck. The crew man in turn threw himself down beside the engine room casing. I was looking toward the bow, which disappeared above the arch of the bridge as it went out of the bridge hole. The underside of the arch was now just above my head. We came out of the bridge, she levelled off and we were away. It was only then that I broke out into a cold sweat. Once again the old river men had been right, for she had pushed the water out of the bridge hole to dip beneath the arch. I would never do that again, not even if someone offered me a thousand pounds.

The farmers and landowners had complained that their land was under water and unworkable for a quarter of the year. In response, the authorities had the banks scraped from Ashleworth to below Gloucester and cleared them of trees, bushes and various other obstacles. When the next floods came, it was like pulling the plug out of the bath. The water just ran away twice as fast as it ever did and the speed of the river had now greatly increased. We left Gloucester one morning at 5 a.m., heading upstream with the Regent Lady and Regent Lord. We towed all that day and into the night. When we got to Chitters Brook below Hamstall, it was approximately four o'clock the next morning and I was at the wheel. It took an hour to tow the dumb barge past one tree against the current. When we eventually arrived on our berth at Stourport it was eight o'clock the following next morning. We had been towing twenty eight hours and still had to discharge and get back with hardly any sleep. My captain telephoned the head office at Gloucester at nine o'clock, as we were still discharging our cargoes. He told them that no way were we able to tow to Stourport-on-Severn again because of the change of the flow and speed of the water. This was the reason the dumb barges became redundant, because it was impossible to continue towing them. From then on, only power craft were used up here to the finish. If one looks at the river banks now it can be seen that they have had to be reinforced with granite blocks about 6ft square to stop erosion of the banks by the speed of the water. So much for the bank clearance scheme.

Before the clearing scheme, we went up the pounds (a length of river between marks), from Worcester to Stourport with great difficulty. Many a wheel house was lost from branches over-hanging the river and not spotted soon enough to avoid them. They would sweep the wheelhouse off, smash it and it would go over the side. So the carpenters at Gloucester had good practice making and fitting new ones. They must have known the measurements off by heart. Consequently, we always had spare steering wheels in the store. These events used to happen because when we got up to this end of the river, night was drawing in and although the motor craft carried head lights, the dumb barges did not. Invariably it was the dumb barges that lost their wheelhouses.

When we arrived at Stourport we had to discharge and swing around for the return journey. The dumb barge had to swing around first, and with the flow and speed of the water, we always carried two special swinging ropes on board for they would come round at a terrific speed, hitting the jetty. We would have fenders ready to bounce off and the ropes had to take all the strain. Once I saw the ropes break and the dumb barge and its crew head down the river. We were unable to catch them with the motor craft. It was only about half a mile to Lincombe Weir and the three men tried to release the lifeboat but did not have enough time. There was only about two feet of flood water at this point and she went broadside onto the weir, bounced on to it then over the edge, dropping about three feet. The three man crew hung on for their lives. The vessel was taken down into trees at the other side and was extensively damaged. Because of our draft on the motor craft we had to lock down at Lincombe Lock, chase after them to catch them and tow them to Holt Lock before we could check the damage. I might say here that these three men were very shaken after this episode.

Always when running the bridges, it was essential to use full speed. If you did not, you would drop under one side of the arch of the bridge you were running, as the Darleydale had. Then you were in trouble. Many bridges have been hit and usually the greatest damage was done to the craft.

If you ever have the chance to go up the River Severn and through the Worcester Road Bridge, do look up and see the evidence of deep gauges and ruts in the stonework. I once lost one side of my wheelhouse because I dropped too far to my starboard side. The wheelhouse was folded down, but was resting on the bollards, so it was propped up a little. The corner caught the bridge and hey presto, glass and timber flew everywhere.

Since the bank clearances, the water does not rise to the heights it used to, but as there are no tankers or cargo craft left to use the river, it does not worry people so much.

Never again will any craft go out of Gloucester docks without locking. On an occasion of record floods, I once took the Regent Jill out of Gloucester dock into the flooded River Severn. The water in the dock and the canal was level with the river and all four lock gates were open. Following me out that day was the 'Regent Lady', then the 'Regent Swift'. The occasion was reported in the Gloucester Citizen and Journal, as it had never been achieved before.

After the three craft had cleared the lock, the lock gates were closed. Then the river stop gates were put into place as the river was still rising, and within the hour it was three inches higher than the dock and canal.

These stop gates were used regularly in those days for it was nothing to see water over the meadows, even covering the island completely from Gloucester dock to the river at Over. This does not happen as it used to. Even today, the water can cover the grounds around Maisemore, Ashleworth, Wainlodes and across to Coombe Hill.

I often wonder what the people of Worcester and Gloucester

would have felt if they had known of the full danger of a tanker in collision with one of the bridges. A tiny spark could have caused a blazing inferno and a major catastrophy. It was due to the skill and knowledge of the tanker men that such a disaster never happened.

Chapter Sixteen

Living off the River

During the years we worked the river we became very adept at both poaching and legitimate fishing. We could live off the river, from fish we could catch with tie lines or fishing rods, or from shooting game. Yes, we did have guns on board, illegal I know, but most craft had one. It was usually hidden between the mattress and the board at the side of the owners bunk.

When we were moored in Avonmouth, a saltwater dock, we used to fish for eels and mullet. It was also illegal to fish here, but it would have been very difficult for anyone to see the tie line moored to the offside of a vessel. As bait for eels, we used bits of meat or even dead mice, and for mullet, lug worm. Some of the eels we caught were up to five and six pounds in weight. We did have some men that were scared of catching hold of the writhing eels to remove them from the hooks. It was hilarious to watch them try.

If we went ashore at Shepperdine we used to go fishing for flat fish, dabs or flatties as they were nicknamed. We used to fish with Mr Percy Palmer the light keeper, who had a small boat and long net. We would change into our swimming costumes, if the weather was warm enough, and get out onto the mud with the end of the net. Percy would then row out into the river, bring the end of the net round back to the shore in a horse-shoe shape and pull it in. Hopefully, with the flat fish and maybe an occasional mullet with it.

At Sharpness around Easter time the elvers arrived in the river, so we carried a special net to catch them. Elvers are baby eels around three inches long and virtually transparent. They were a delicacy that we used to catch with a meat sieve attached to a broom handle. We used to catch them until they had begun to turn colour because we believed they weren't so good to eat at this stage. Nowadays elvers command very high prices and they are fished for over months. In my opinion, they will over fish these creatures until they are extinct. We were lucky, as we could catch our elvers on low tides at Sharpness. They could not usually get above Gloucester because most tides did not cover Gloucester Weir. Being aboard these tankers we had the best of both worlds, for when they sometimes did go up over the weir at Gloucester on higher tides of about 24ft at Sharpness, we could catch them up there. The men on shore at Sharpness had to wait for the neap or low tides to catch them again at Sharpness.

On the canal, we used to fish for eels with night lines baited mainly with gudgeon caught with rod and line. We have caught an occasional bream or roach for cooking, but prepared very carefully, otherwise they would taste earthy.

When we locked out of Gloucester and proceeded up the river, ducks, pheasant, hares, rabbits; and eels, lampreys, salmon and other fish were all fair game. Each vessel carried a net for scooping up any ducks that were shot. This was usually a bicycle wheel rim with a net fixed to it and attached to a long pole. If a hare, rabbit or pheasant was shot, a man was put ashore to pick it up.

Many a salmon has been caught basking in the sun on a shallow. The vessel going by would pull the water from its pool, leaving the fish high and dry. The water would then come back with such force it would throw the salmon much higher up the bank. Upon which, a tankerman would leap ashore, sprint back and claim the salmon quicker than you could say 'Jack Robinson'. Well yes, maybe it was poaching, but then you had to be caught didn't you?

Rabbits and hares were regular targets and often ended in the pot. When the floods used to cover the banks, there were small islands of land left, sometimes there were rabbits or hares marooned on them. We could get ashore, wade to the island and catch them by hand, using the improvised landing net, and a winch bar as a truncheon.

Lampreys, we could get quite easily from our small craft for they used to attach themselves to the weir at Camp or Bevere. Here all we had to do, was to scoop them into a net, transfer them to a sand bag, and there was another good meal for us.

Often we have moored to a bank to go mushrooming. On a moonlight night it not unusual for a tanker to be moored without lights and the crew ashore helping themselves to a feed or two of mushrooms, having left one man aboard to see that the ship was OK.

Also, I have known a farmer and his pickers, gathering sprouts at one end of a field and the crew of a tanker picking at the other end but on their hands and knees so as not to be seen.

In the autumn, a tanker would moor up in the early hours of the morning alongside an orchard and the crew jump ashore to help themselves to the fruit. For all the years I was aboard these vessels I never heard of anyone getting caught.

Another way of poaching salmon was to sit on the side of an island armed with an air rifle alongside the salmon jump. These were pools at the end of a weir built on the island side of a weir for the fish to jump up the weir to continue up river to the spawning ground.

Many is the man that had sat hidden in the bushes, unbeknown to the lock keeper or bailiff, and as the salmon jumped up into the pools, he has shot and spirited it away.

Pike was another fish that could be hand caught, I have stalked a pike on a summer's day in Lincombe bottom cutting, on what is known as the old river entrance, and is a sand bank. I spotted this fish in about a foot of water basking under the old bridge. I borrowed a gaff, walked down the bank from the lock, took my shoes and socks off, rolled up my trousers and then stepped into the water. As I moved very, very slowly out to the fish, I held the gaff out in front of me with the hook pointing downward. When I was far enough over it, I brought the gaff down in a sweeping motion catching the fish in the tail. I ran ashore, dropped it onto the bank and killed it with my shoe. Another one for the pot, a nice seven pound Jack pike.

I remember two brothers on board the same craft. They owned a single barrel twelve bore gun that had a broken trigger. Undeterred, they decided to have a shot at a duck. They put a cartridge into the barrel and prepared to shoot. Their system was, for the one brother to hold and point the gun and the other, on command, struck the hammer of the gun with a spanner. So engrossed in watching the ducks was the one with the spanner, that when his brother said 'hit it'. He missed and clouted him on the back of his ear. The air turned blue, the ducks lived for another day and everyone on board fell about laughing.

Another mishap I was told about; a man ran up the companion way steps holding his gun by the barrel. Unfortunately, it was loaded and somehow the gun went off. Luckily the shot hit the metal bulkhead, ricocheted off and about five or six pellets embedded themselves under the skin of his thigh. He then had to lay on his bunk whilst a crewman dug them out with a sharp penknife.

A most dangerous accident was in the cabin of one of the old vessels and it was very lucky no one was hurt. The deck boy had just finished washing himself and stood combing his hair. He was looking into a mirror, which hung from a bar down the front of a forty gallon fresh water tank that was bolted to the fore bulk head in the cabin. The signal was given that there were some ducks in the offing. The crew member who owned the gun was sitting on the edge of his bunk that was made fast to the after bulk head. The gun was opened, a cartridge put in, the gun was snapped shut. The gun spontaniously fired and the glass the boy was looking into was shattered, not a foot from his face. It shook both of them so much no more guns were loaded in the cabin by that man again, although he still kept a gun on board.

I have been told tales of what went on before my time, of the old longboat men catching and eating half grown cygnets. Whether this was true I don't know, but I believe that it could have been. I have seen an old long boatman take a cygnet out of a family of five cygnets with the old swans in attendance. The old cob went absolutely berserk until the cygnet was put back in the water.

Living off the river did not only apply just to the tanker men but also the general cargo men, for a good river man worth his salt was also a good provider. The old longboatmen back in the days of horse drawn longboats, lived with their families on board and had to provide for them. It was a skill handed down through the ages.

Chapter Seventeen

The Finish

During my Severn tanking years, I saw many men come and go. Some of them might only work for a week or two, unable to stand the pace. Some of them may have stayed a year or two, or see one winter through and then go because it was too hard a life. But the worse than that, not only did the men go, but the craft started to diminish as well. Of course, this all happened in my later years. If anyone had said to me in 1940 that all this would be finished in thirty years time, I would have laughed at them. But it did, and when I think back to the many vessels and their crews that came and went, it makes me feel quite sad.

From boy to man I made many friends from all over the country, even the Scandinavian countries. There were also many men who came from Yorkshire with their small craft owned by J. Harkers of Knottingley. Some were married, some were single. Many single men married girls from this area and settled here. Alas, there are no tank craft left.

As the depots started to be run down at Gloucester, Worcester, and Stourport so the tankers became less and less. In the beginning it was gradual, just one or two now and then sold for scrap. Some were sent back around the coast to Yorkshire and some to the other rivers to see if they could make a go of it elsewhere. As roads got wider and faster, lorries took over the general cargo trade. Then some of our fleet were sold and not replaced. The dumb barges went first, then the Regents Jill, Lady and Queen. By this time most of the Harker tankers had gone, there were just a few of the larger ones running to Worcester.

A lot of the tankers were scrapped. Some were sold to continental firms, some went to Ireland and some were sold to work at other tasks in our own waters. For instance, the 'Regent Robin' was altered into a Sand Sucking barge to be used in the Southampton water I believe, and was renamed the 'Sand Robin'.

The disused jetties at Stourport-on-Severn, photo taken in 1984.

Then one day, when I was Master of The Regent Lark, I arrived empty back at Gloucester from Stourport. I moored in the Monk Meadow Oil dock and walked into the office with my ship's papers. I was called into the Manager's office where I was informed that my vessel the Regent Lark had been sold to a Dutch firm. I was told to instruct my crew to get their gear off as soon as they could. I had been allocated the Regent Swift to carry on the work that was left. By this time vessels were being moored up, put up for sale and their crews laid off because of the lack of work. This brought a feeling of sickness to all that were left. We were now asking ourselves how long would we last? As the craft were moored up, the old hands were put on board other craft replacing the newer hands that had to go first. Some men found other jobs on shore and left. There were about seven of us that stayed to the end, aboard the only three craft left that were working. The Regent Wren running to Gloucester and the Regent Robin and Swift to Stourport. Then very suddenly, they were moored up with the others in the old dock at Sharpness until they were sold.

The old war time pipe lines helped to finish us off as well. As technology improved, the oil companies were able to pump all sorts of grades of oil and fuel, one after the other without mixing them, through these pipe lines. They still do this and with the pipe line system oil companies can pump all over the country cutting costs dramatically. For instance, oil can be pumped from Avonmouth to Birmingham, London and many other larger cities, cutting the freight charges of the roads, canals and rivers.

We all knew then that we were finished. For us the river had died. A sad, sad day. We loved the river and had worked on the Severn from as young as sixteen. The last few of us left had all been there since boyhood, and were all in our forties. Some used to say that it would come back, but our hearts knew different. I am lucky because I still see the river at Sharpness, Worcester and Stourport. I married a Stourport girl and we still visit there where I sometimes walk on the Red Cliff overlooking the old depots and I can look up and down the river and remember the old days. That is all that is left for me of the River Severn tanking life, but I still call and meet many of the friends that I made during these very good, very hard years.

I still wish that the life, although hard, had not finished. Because even after all these years ashore, I believe I would go back to working on the river. I know that there are other river men that would do the same, but they know as I do that this will never happen. Severn tanking is, I am sorry to say, finished for ever.